The Dog Who Came to Stay
A Memoir

Hal Borland

With an introduction by Les Line

THE LYONS PRESS
Guilford, Connecticut
An imprint of The Globe Pequot Press

For Barbara:
The one woman in Pat's life
and in mine

First Lyons Press edition, 2003

The Lyons Press is an imprint of The Globe Pequot Press.

10 9 8 7 6 5 4 3 2 1

Printed in the United States of America

ISBN 1-59228-065-X

Library of Congress Cataloging-in-Publication Data
is available on file.

INTRODUCTION

Hal Borland was one of America's most beloved nature writers—a genre that thrived in the mid-20th century but teeters on the brink of extinction in today's literary world. In 1968 he won the coveted John Burroughs Medal for Distinguished Nature Writing and a few years later he was honored by nature education professionals with the Interpretative Naturalists' Award. After his death in 1978, the National Audubon Society established the Hal Borland Award "to recognize lasting contributions to the understanding, appreciation and protection of nature through writing, photography or art."

Reviewers would note the poetic, contemplative quality of Borland's writing and compared him favorably to Henry David Thoreau. Indeed, as he told *Contemporary Authors*, "I am often called a naturalist because I have written a good deal about the natural world. I have a certain competence in that field, but I think of myself as a natural philosopher; I am interested in life, all kinds of life, and must consider it in the framework of this natural world."

In fact, "nature writer" is too confining a term, by far, to describe Borland. A prolific author for more than forty years, his oeuvre includes, in addition to his many natural history titles, critically acclaimed fiction for both adults and young readers; autobiographical books that vividly recall a lost slice of Americana; a how-to book on writing and selling non-fiction; and even Western novels with titles like *Rustler's Trail* written under the pen name Ward West.

And then there were his dog stories, children's books about canines named Valor and Penny and this enduring classic for grownups featuring Pat, "The Dog Who Came to Stay." Said a *New York Times* reviewer in 1961, "Pat's story will appeal to all people who have ever been closely attached to a dog. This book will delight, too, Mr. Borland's many readers who have enjoyed his reflection on country ways and the seasonal changes. But make no mistake, Pat is always at stage center, a 'notional dog' as a neighbor called him."

That immense interest in the natural world and country ways came inherently, for Harold Glen Borland was a child of the American frontier. He was born in 1900 in Sterling, Nebraska, close by a fork of the Oregon Trail, where his blacksmith grandfather had settled to set up a forge and build a mill. "He made nails and hinges for the village church, built wagons that would last a farmer's lifetime, fed, clothed and schooled a big family, and died in his fifties," Borland wrote in *High, Wide and Lonesome,* the first of two marvelous books about his youth. "Two of his sons became blacksmiths, two became railroad men, one became a teacher, one the local sexton, one an editor."

The editor was Hal's father, Will Borland, who also tried the smithy's trade but strode out of the shop after a few months and apprenticed himself to the village printer, becoming a master printer and part-owner of the town's weekly paper. However, like Borland men of several generations past, Will succumbed to the westward urge. So in the spring of 1910 he took his family to the plains of Colorado and settled on a homestead some distance south of the Platte River where the closest neighbor to their sod house was two miles away, the nearest post office twelve miles off, and if you needed a doctor it was a thirty-mile wagon ride.

Will discovered, though, that he wasn't much of a farmer and in 1915 the Borlands moved to Flagler, a new, growing Colorado town of about 750 people with a struggling newspaper. "Father bought the *Flagler News* and became a distinguished country editor," Hal recounted. "There, under him, I learned the printer's trade just as I always knew he wanted me to. There I went to high school. And I went to the state university from there, along with the son of a man who had trailed a herd of longhorns up the Chisholm Trail from Texas and a boy whose father had once hunted buffalo. And I came to know that a frontier is never a place; it is a time and a way of life. I came to know that frontiers pass, but they endure in their people."

It was natural, too, that Borland followed his father into newspapering, working alongside him at the Flagler journal after college before moving to New York City and jobs with the long-lost *Brooklyn Times,* United Press and then King Features. Over the next several years a rather peripatetic journalism career would lead him to a string of cities around the West before Borland settled in Philadelphia in 1927, becoming literary editor for both the morning and evening *Ledger.* Then in 1937 he moved back to Manhattan as a staff writer for *The New York Times*

Sunday magazine. In 1941 he submitted a short essay on the English oak to the paper's editorial page, and his path soon took the first of two definitive turns. An "outdoor editorial" by Borland became a fixture in the Sunday *Times*—they would eventually number 1,750—and the life of a freelance beckoned in 1943. For the next eight years Borland worked from his home "at the edge of the country" in Connecticut suburbs, traveling "wherever an editor sent me, making a living at my typewriter."

"All that time," he continued, "I had made occasion, at least once a week, to renew my acquaintance with the trees and flowers, the weather and the wind. However, I felt the need to remain close to the city, never more than an hour away. The habit was deeply ingrained, and though I compromised by owning a few acres of hillside and brook and coming to know them intimately, I was being trapped by suburbanization, which in its own way is worse than urbanization."

A near-fatal illness freed Borland from that trap. Reappraising their life, he and his wife Barbara agreed "that there were things more important than an assignment in Maine or Tennessee. She, too, felt that a self-chosen assignment on a hillside of my own choosing was the important thing now."

So in July 1952 the Borlands bought a farmhouse and one hundred acres—"one whole side of a mountain and half a mile of river bank"—in the far northwestern corner of Connecticut, a brisk walk from the Massachusetts line and a wonderful nature preserve called Bartholomew's Cobble. And on the Borland's first Christmas at Weatogue, as their little valley is known (from a Mahican Indian word meaning "home"), Pat, a black-and-white part-foxhound, came to stay, announcing his intentions at midnight, in the midst of a snowstorm, by howling near the Borland's bedroom window.

"How is it," Borland asked in the early pages of Pat's book, "that hurt, lost creatures turn, as though by instinct, to a haven. Do they sense warmth and food and friendly protection? Do they know where soft-hearted people live, and seek them out? Pat certainly found a welcome home at Weatogue, and it's delightful to have his story back in print.

Les Line was editor of *Audubon* magazine from 1966 to 1991 and his photographs accompanied Hal Borland essays in three books: *Seasons, A Countryman's Flowers,* and *A Countryman's Woods.* He is a field editor for *National Wildlife* magazine, contributes to several other magazines as well as the science pages of *The New York Times,* and is the author, photographer or editor of more than thirty books including the recent *Speaking for Nature: A Century of Conservation.*

CHAPTER 1

THE DOGS came on Christmas night and were even more un-welcome than the weather, which had turned windy and wild with sleety snow riding the gale. We expect snow up here in the hills by Christmas, but we don't expect strange dogs to drop in, especially in the winter.

It was our first winter on the farm in this part of the upper Housatonic Valley called Weatogue. It lies in the edge of the Berkshires, in the extreme northwest corner of Connecticut; the Massachusetts line is only a little more than a mile up the road, and New York State is only a couple of hills and valleys to the west. Both north and south of us are summer vacation areas but, thanks to Yankee stubbornness, this remains a rural valley of working farms. Albert, our nearest neighbor, is a dairy farmer who lives a long half-mile down the road. Charley, another dairy-man and our neighbor up the road, lives a mile away. From where we live, there isn't another house in sight. But just over the hills to the east, five miles by winding road but close enough by crow-flight that we can often hear its church bells, is the old village of Canaan. Salisbury village, equally old, is five miles to the south of us.

So we live here in the privacy of pastureland, mountainside, and river. The Housatonic flows just beyond the dooryard, and Tom's Mountain, a rugged, rocky knob on a long ridge of tim-bered ledges, rises abruptly a few hundred yards behind the house, just beyond the strip of pastureland.

We own a hundred acres "more or less," as the deed says cau-tiously. Its boundaries are stated in terms of stone walls, big oak trees and certain large rocks, all of which may or may not still be there, for the terms of the deed date back to the eighteenth century. I have been able to identify only a few of the landmarks, and at least a dozen are listed. The outlines of this property seem to resemble the random scissor work of a five-year-old trying to cut a five-point star from a sheet of paper with dull scissors. But it really doesn't matter, to us. We came here to live with the land, not off it, and such boundaries are not too important.

We came here in July, and we had little more than settled in before fall was upon us. Fall was long and mild, as New England autumns so often are. It came with frosty nights in September, it flamed into the October glory of the woodlands, and it eased into the blue skies and wide horizons of November. Two light, fluffy snows fell, barely enough to whiten the grass and hold for a few hours the tracks of cottontails, gray squirrels, a fox or two, and a herd of deer. Thanksgiving was shirt-sleeve mild. Early December was like a dividend from November and Christmas week arrived green, as we say. Actually it was brown and tan and gray, the brown and bare cornfields, the tan of sere pastures, the silvery gray of naked maples. The only green was in the pines and hemlocks that clothe the upper half of the mountain.

The day before Christmas Barbara said we should have some green in the house. "Our own greenery." So we went part way up the mountain and brought back a small white pine, an armload of hemlock boughs, and a few handfuls of ground cedar and partridge berry.

Christmas morning we sat in front of the open fire in the Franklin stove and opened the gifts that had come by mail. The little tree in the corner of the living room winked with lights and tinsel balls. Hemlock boughs with big red bows hung in the windows. The bookcases were festooned with ground cedar and strands of partridge berry. Just outside the house, making the whole place look like a Christmas card, stood the giant Norway spruce, bigger than any municipal tree ever hauled in from the far hills.

We opened the gifts and had toast and coffee in front of the fire, and we felt snug and content. We were two writers who had been wanderers and had now begun to put down roots. Barbara, a native New Englander, had been a city girl much of her life. I was a native Westerner who grew up in the country but had worked in city offices for years before I quit a daily desk job. We had come here from two suburban acres and a house with neighbors just beyond the dooryard.

I said I wished there were a lot of pretties for Barbara that Christmas, and I promised that there would be next Christmas. She said she wished there were boots and guns and fishing tackle for me, and made promises too. Then we looked around us and she said, "We've got the important gifts, both of us, right now. The river, the mountainside—this whole place! And we're almost well again."

That was the best gift of all, health. Earlier that year I had several months of critical illness, and the strain of that time almost put Barbara in the hospital too. But it wasn't a "carrying-off disease," as we said, and when I began to recover we decided to simplify our lives and get back to enduring things, to the land. So we bought this place, packed up our typewriters and moved.

I sat on the floor, that morning, feeding the Christmas wrappings into the fire, and Barbara salvaged gay ribbons, and we laughed at the memory of the warnings of our urban friends. They had said this place was as isolated as Patagonia, practically a primitive area, and that we would get cabin-fever in the winter, *if* we survived. They had their wry amusement, but we had our own answers. The place is a hundred-odd miles from New York City; but even in the suburbs we went to the city only occasionally. We wouldn't miss the city. The house is snug and equipped with all essential utilities, most of them stormproof; it is in no sense primitive living. As for isolation, a writer needs privacy. And winter can get tiresome anywhere, but there is both beauty and excitement in a rural winter. We saw few hazards and many advantages. I grew up in the country, far more primitive country than this, so we weren't exactly babes in the New England woods.

We were reviewing all this and telling ourselves that we had chosen wisely in making the move, when a car drew up and a big man in dungarees, denim jacket and red winter cap came to the door. It was Charley, our neighbor from up the road. I went to the door and he shouted, "Merry Christmas!" and came in and looked around. "Well!" he exclaimed. "You went up on the hill and got yourself a tree."

"We went up as far as the pines," I said. "Both of us."

"You couldn't have got that far when you first came here," Charley said as he sat down. "By next fall you'll be out getting your own venison. I got me a fat doe yesterday. You like venison?"

I said, "Yes. But it's been a long time."

"I'll bring you a couple of steaks." He turned to Barbara. "Venison's a dry meat. Fry it in plenty of butter and don't cook it too long. That makes it tough." He turned back to me. "If we had a good rabbit dog we'd go out after rabbits. My Poochy's a good coon dog, but no good on rabbits. Maybe you'll get a rabbit dog."

"Maybe." A dog didn't fit into our plans. We had begun to put down roots, but no telling when an editor would ask us to go to some far place on an assignment. Then what would we do with a dog, if we had one? No need to go into that with Charley, though.

"I've got a dog up at the house," Charley was saying, "that used to be one of the best rabbit dogs around. But he's old and half blind now. Just lies in back of the kitchen stove and sleeps. Frank Snyder's old dog." He paused for a moment. "We buried Frank day before yesterday. He asked us to look after his dog when they took him to the hospital. It was the last thing we could do for him."

Frank Snyder once owned this farm, but I never met him. He sold the place some years back and was only a name to me. I had heard that he was old and sick but I didn't know that he had died. Charley's wife, Elitha, was related to the Snyders and had been raised by Frank and his wife.

Charley talked about him, about the years when the Snyders lived here and about the transient marks any man leaves on the land. The stone walls in the pastures and on the mountain were laid up long before Frank Snyder was born, since the white man's taming of this valley began in 1738; but he stripped one pasture wall for stones to make a foundation for the big chicken house. He kept open several roads up the mountain and farmed a few fields up there; but now the roads were gullied and overgrown and the old mountainside fields were thickets of gray birch, white ash and sumac. Like others before him, he tapped the big maples just across the road from the house and made syrup and sugar; but the holes he bored for the spiles had long ago healed to faint scars on the rough gray bark.

"He used to fish," Charley finally said, "and he used to hunt

10

foxes up on the hill. But I guess the pickerel and the foxes have forgotten him by now. That's the way it goes."

He stood up to leave, but he paused long enough to ask, "Do you think a man's dog knows when he dies?"

I hesitated, thinking of the white collie.

Charley didn't wait for an answer. "The day Frank Snyder died," he said, "his dog howled. Twice. Right there in the kitchen. Even before we got word. Hasn't been a yelp out of him since." He shook his head, puzzled.

We went out onto the porch. "Warm for this time of year," I said.

"Too warm. And we need snow." He glanced at the sky. "But weather's breeding. If the wind shifts, we'll get a storm tonight."

The wind shifted early that afternoon. We went for our daily walk up the road about three o'clock, and before we turned back the wind had a bite. It gusted up the valley and stung our faces, and before we reached the house there was a spit of sleety snow in the air. By dusk pellet snow rattled at the windowpanes. We ate supper and sat by the fire and read for a time and went to bed early, thankful for a warm house. The storm was still building up.

It was around midnight when I wakened. I lay listening to the beat of the storm, which rattled the windows, swished in the maples and moaned in the giant spruce. Then I heard the sound that had awakened me. A dog howled, close beside the house.

A dog howling in the night, any night but particularly a stormy winter night, can raise my hackles. It's a primitive sound, a wail right out of the wilderness. I lay and listened, and hoped it wouldn't waken Barbara. Then I heard her sharp intake of breath and she asked in a tense whisper, "What's that?"

"The wind," I suggested, hoping the dog wouldn't howl again. But it did.

"It's a dog!" Then, "Or a wolf?"

"A dog. Just a dog."

"Whose dog?"

"I don't know. Some dog going down the road."

Silence for a long moment. Then she whispered, "It's Mr. Snyder's dog."

"No. Charley wouldn't let a dog out on a night like this."

But, to reassure her, I got out of bed and went to the window. I couldn't see a thing. The wind wailed in the maples and the air was icy. But I stood there at the window for a minute or two, thinking of Frank Snyder. A man and his dog. The dog didn't howl again and I went back to bed.

"Whatever it was," I said, "it's gone now."

"It was his dog," Barbara murmured, already drifting back to sleep. I listened to her regular breathing, but I lay awake. And I remembered the white collie.

As a boy I had a cross-bred sable collie named Fritz. I brought him home in my hat, he a puppy only a few weeks old, and he and I grew up together on the Colorado plains. Then I went away to college and I went to work and Fritz became my father's dog. They were companions for five or six years, and the collie's death was a deeper blow to my father than it was to me, for I was far away at the time.

Fritz had been dead almost twenty years when my mother sent word that my father was mortally ill. Barbara and I hurried half across the continent to the little Colorado plains town, and Father seemed to rally new strength for us though it was obvious that he didn't have a chance. But we had an afternoon and evening with him, a happy time. Father was full of reminiscence and he spoke with special fondness of Fritz, the collie. About three o'clock the next morning my father died.

A little later, at the first streaks of dawn, Barbara and I set out on foot for the railroad depot to send telegrams. At the first corner of the sleeping town we were joined by a pure white collie. He came trotting up to us and licked my hand and walked beside me, just as Fritz had walked in my boyhood. He went to the depot with us and waited while we sent the messages and walked back to the house with us. At the front steps he hesitated, and when I looked again he was gone. I never saw him again.

Later that day I asked who in town had a white collie. My question met blank looks. There wasn't a white collie in town, or any other pure white dog. And I asked no more questions. There are some things you don't pursue too far.

I lay there, that Christmas night after the howling dog had wakened me, and I thought of Frank Snyder and his old dog, and

I thought of my father and the white collie, and I listened to the storm. And finally I, too, went back to sleep.

At breakfast the next morning Barbara and I both asked the same question: "Was it a dream, or did a howling dog wake you up last night?"

No, it wasn't a dream. We had both heard it. But in full daylight we could laugh about it, even as we wondered. You hear strange things in the night, and the darkness sometimes invests them with strange meaning. We spoke of Frank Snyder's dog, and we dismissed it. Then I spoke of the white collie. Barbara remembered. And finally, to make sure, to clarify our minds and rule out imagination, I phoned Charley's house. Elitha answered.

"No," she said, "it couldn't have been the old dog. He was in the house all night. He's here right now, sleeping behind the stove. . . . No, it couldn't have been Poochy either. He's been in all night too. It wasn't a fit night out for man *or* dog. Today's nothing to brag about either. I wish it would quit blowing and settle down and snow, if it's going to."

We hung up and I told Barbara what Elitha had said. Then, out of curiosity, I went to the front door. There was less than an inch of snow, and it was still blowing a gale, but maybe if I looked I could find tracks in some sheltered place around the house.

I stepped out onto the porch and there was a scurry in a corner. Two dogs scrambled past me and dashed down the steps. They fled around the house. All I saw was that one was black and the other was black and white.

I came back inside and Barbara and I watched from a window as the dogs skirted the woodshed and started across the pasture. The black one turned, looked at the house, lifted its head and howled. Then they went on across the pasture and into the brushy margin at the foot of the mountain.

"There," I said, "is our night-howler." And I went back to the porch and found the bare spot in the corner where they had lain, somewhat shielded from the storm, most of the night. Two strays who had wandered in from somewhere, found temporary shelter, and now had gone on.

Later in the morning Charley stopped in with a packet of venison chops. I described the dogs to him, one a long-haired black

13

pup, apparently, the other a black and white spotted hound. "Both," I said, "were rib-thin, starved."

Charley shook his head. "No dogs like that around here. They must be strays. I hope they aren't deer-chasers."

The spitting snow stopped by mid-morning, but the wind continued raw and gusty. We bundled up for our afternoon walk, but we could face that wire-edged wind only about ten minutes. We turned back, and before we reached the house the snow was falling again, this time big, soft flakes, and the wind had begun to ease.

We came up the steps and there were the two dogs again. They had been huddled in the sheltered corner, as before, but when they heard us they leaped to their feet, stood shivering for a moment, then dashed past us, down the steps, around the house and across the pasture into the brush once more.

We came inside, and Barbara asked, "What are we going to do about them?"

"Do?" I said. "There's nothing to do. They don't belong to us."

"They are hungry. And cold."

"If we feed them they'll settle down here and we'll have a couple of dogs."

"Someone should feed them. They must belong somewhere."

"I thought you didn't like dogs. Remember the big white ones?"

"Bears!" she exclaimed. "They were big as bears! These are —they're just dogs. Dog-size dogs."

Six weeks earlier I had left the car in the driveway till after dark one evening. When I went out to put it away in the garage two huge, shadowy creatures lumbered up to me, startling me in the darkness. They were Great Pyrenees, big as Newfoundlands and friendly as puppies. Their cream-colored coats were ghostly in the darkness. They came to me and I patted them, and I put the car away.

When I returned to the house they padded along with me, one on each side, and when I opened the door one of them pushed in ahead of me and went down the hallway and into the kitchen before I could get there. I shouted a warning, but too late. I give Barbara credit. She didn't scream. But after I caught up with that great, shaggy creature and threw him out she said she thought it was a polar bear and didn't know whether to stab it with a cooking fork or turn and run. I chased the big fellow out and he and his companion must have gone back to their owner in the village five miles away. We didn't see them around here again.

"These," she said now, "are just dogs." And she went to the phone and called every house in the valley. Nobody had lost a dog. Nobody had ever seen the dogs she described.

A little later I looked out on the porch. No dogs. I said hopefully, "We've probably seen the last of them."

We hadn't. They were back that night, and again they wakened us with their howling. And the next morning they were there on the porch. When I opened the door they leaped up, as usual, went around the house and off across the pasture.

After breakfast I decided to see where they were staying, up there in the brush. I put on boots and a heavy coat and followed their tracks. The tracks led through the fringe of brush and into a tight clump of pasture cedars at the foot of the mountain. There were the dogs, shivering in the dry grass. I called to them, tried to make friends. They would have none of me. The little black one was of two minds, but the black and white one left the cedars and retreated on up the hillside, and the black one followed. I gave up and came back to the house. They followed me, fifty yards behind, and before I had taken off my coat and boots, there they were on the porch again.

We stood at a front window and watched them huddle down together. "Do you suppose the spotted one is the black one's mother?" Barbara asked.

"Both males," I said.

"Father and son, then?"

"Different breeds. The black one has setter blood and the black and white one's at least part foxhound."

"They're awfully thin."

But I refused to get sentimental about two tramp dogs. I did the morning chores and went to my typewriter.

We had steak for dinner. Barbara denies it, but I still think she deliberately went through the steaks in the freezer and picked the one with the biggest bone and most gristle. When we had finished, there was that big bone and all the fat and gristly scraps. She looked at the scraps, then at me. I shook my head, but she said, "You aren't half as tough as you pretend." She put the bone and the scraps on an old pie tin, and I took them outside.

Only one dog was there, the black and white hound. He smelled the meat and looked at me, hungry and shivering, his nose twitching. But when I approached him he scuttled down the steps. He stood there in the yard, trembling, that mouth-watering smell still in his nostrils. I went down and set the pan in the snow. He backed away, and I returned to the porch.

He watched me for a long moment, then approached the pan, one wary step at a time, eying me. He grabbed a chunk of fatty gristle and gulped it. He wolfed another chunk, then picked up the bone. The black pup came around the corner of the house and I expected a fight over the bone. Instead, the spotted hound put down the bone and stood aside. The black pup grabbed it and began to gnaw as though he hadn't eaten in a month. The black and white hound stood on guard, watching me, while the pup gnawed the bone clean.

I came into the house. Barbara had been watching from the window. "Did you ever see that happen before?" she asked.

"Never."

"These," she said, "are unusual dogs."

"Tramps!"

When we went for our afternoon walk the dogs, instead of dashing off across the pasture and into the brush, followed us up the road. When we came back they followed us home and settled down on the porch again. It was bitter cold outside, warm in the house. As I took off my coat I knew that I could be tough just so long. I said, "How much milk have we got?"

"Only one quart."

"I've got to go to the village anyway. I'm almost out of pipe tobacco."

She brought the milk and put it in a pan to heat. She set out the last loaf of bread. I crumbled the bread into the warm milk and set it out for the dogs. It was gone in a dozen mouthfuls. I thought the dogs were going to lick a hole in the bottom of the pan.

I went to the telephone.

"What are you going to do?" Barbara asked.

"Call the dog warden."

"Why?"

"See if he has any report of missing dogs."

"What if he hasn't?"

"He'll come get them and dispose of them."

"Destroy them?"

"Look," I said, "you can't have tramp dogs running loose, vandals on the countryside."

"So, you feed them, and then call the dog warden!"

I phoned the warden. The only missing dog he had listed was a one-eyed blue-tick hound. I described these two, told him the story.

"You could take them in," he said, "and advertise them. If you don't get an answer to your ad—"

I knew. If there was no answer we would have two dogs. I said, "I may call you back," and I hung up.

"Well?" Barbara asked.

I didn't answer. I went to the door and called the dogs. Everything that happened seemed to be throwing those two dogs into our lap. But before I took another step I wanted to know how they would act in the house, with people.

I called them. The black and white hound scurried down the steps into the yard, but the black pup stood and watched me. I was tempted to shut the door and be done with the whole thing, but the bitter wind was rising again and snow was in the air. It was going to be another of those nights. "Not fit for man *or* dog." I called to the black pup and he wagged a cautious tail and came toward me, step by hesitant step. He smelled the warmth inside. He came to the door, into the hallway. He looked around and whined.

I was still at the open doorway. The black and white hound heard the whine, perked his ears and came slowly up the steps. Watching me, walking almost on tiptoe, he came to the door, looked inside, tense, wary. Then he, too, came in. The two of them went into the living room, crossed to the Navaho rug in front of the open fire. I closed the door. The black pup lay down in front of the fire, sighed, stretched out as though he belonged there. The spotted hound stood for a few minutes, watching us, then lay down with his head on the pup's flank, still on guard.

We sat down and watched them. The black pup slept. The hound closed his eyes, but every time I moved he opened his eyes and looked at me. At last I said, "They'll have to sleep in the woodshed."

"They can have the old brown throw-rug in the attic. Will they be warm enough out there?"

"Warmer than they've been out on the porch."

"The black and white one is still shivering."

"Nervous. Ready to run if we make one quick move."

"Blackie's already settled down."

"Black Mike," I said, "would sell his soul for a bone and a bed."

"Mike!" Barbara exclaimed. "You've named them! Pat and Mike!" Then she said, "It was Christmas night when they came, so they're a Christmas present. I never had a dog. I hope they like me."

"Don't get your hopes up. They may not stay. We've got to advertise them, and someone may answer the ad. Probably will."

I went to get my coat and boots. The black and white hound, the one we had just named Pat, jerked to his feet, watching me. Mike, the black pup, opened his eyes but didn't get up.

"Where are you going?" Barbara asked.

"To the village. What do we need besides bread and milk?"

"Bacon. I think that's all."

I called to the dogs. They got to their feet.

"Are you going to take them with you?"

"No. They're going outdoors till I get back. We still don't know them and I'm not leaving them in here with you alone. Come on, dogs, out with you!"

"What if they run away?"

I laughed. "You couldn't *drive* them away, now. If they should go, though, I'll take the bag of dog food back tomorrow."

She smiled. "Don't forget your pipe tobacco. That's why you have to go to the store. Remember?"

The dogs went outside with me. They were still there on the porch as I backed the car out of the garage and headed for the village. As I drove through the sheeting snow in the lowering dusk

I wondered how it is that hurt, lost creatures turn, as though by instinct, to a haven. Do they sense warmth and food and friendly protection? Do they know where soft-hearted people live, and seek them out?

CHAPTER 2

THE ADVERTISEMENTS brought no answers. Nobody in the whole area, apparently, had lost a black pup or a black and white hound. They wore no collars, had no registration tags, but they could have come from New York, Massachusetts or half a dozen nearby Connecticut townships. I asked everyone I knew, but nobody had ever seen the dogs before, not even skulking across the fields or raiding back-door garbage cans. It was as though they had come out of nowhere, with no history behind them. But wherever they came from, it had been a long, hungry journey.

We mixed panful after panful of warm dog-food mush and watched them gulp it down. That first evening they ate so much I thought they would burst. Then they came inside and lay in front of the fire and groaned in their sleep. When we went to bed they went to the woodshed and curled up on the old rug, and they probably groaned all night. But they didn't howl. The next morning they roamed the fields for an hour, came back and stuffed themselves, lay for a time, went outside for another hour's run, and came back and ate again. When they went with us for the afternoon walk they looked as pot-bellied as starving, rickety children. They were hungry again at suppertime.

It was the fourth day before we began to catch up with their appetites. After that the gullies between their ribs showed signs of filling up, and by the end of the week they were down to three meals a day. But it was several weeks before they tapered off to a normal diet. After that they got a handful of corn flakes in diluted canned milk for breakfast, to take the edge off their appetites and minimize their foraging, and a full meal at suppertime.

The mutual relationship between a dog and a household is a rather subtle matter. It varies, of course, with the personalities involved, with their habits and ways of life and their mutual needs. Most dogs come into a household as puppies or, if they are grown, as relatively known quantities. The pup grows up adapting to an established way of life and trained in the ways that best fit into that life. The grown dog's background is usually taken into account and the advice of the breeder or previous owner can be followed or adapted.

But here were two totally strange dogs, with no known background, coming into a household that neither expected nor really wanted them. Pat, the black and white hound, was an adult dog. I guessed his age at about four years. Pat's habits were established, his character already formed. Mike, the black pup, was probably about a year old. His habits, while less firmly established, were already formed, and he had his own personality. Barbara and I were accustomed to living our own lives and having our house to ourselves. We had never had a dog in our household, and now we had two.

At first we told ourselves that the dogs weren't going to stay. Even though there was no response to the ads, someone would eventually claim them. Meanwhile, we wouldn't become too attached to them. We would see that they had food and shelter and give them a minimum of attention until their owner appeared. There would be no sentiment about them, no nonsense.

Pat's attitude indicated that he felt the same way. He acted the courteous, well-mannered guest, accepting comfort and a certain amount of attention but never demanding them. He wasn't exactly blasé, but he was a dog-of-the-world. He had been around. Mike, on the other hand, was full of young eagerness and emotion. He yelped with joy and he howled with heartbreak. He had no notion of being a guest, anywhere. He made himself at home, immediately and completely, wherever he set foot and found anything approximating a welcome.

Toward the end of the first week Barbara said, "Pat is a gentleman. Just watch the way he walks." We were out for the afternoon walk and Pat trotted along head high, tail up, self-proud and independent. He kept a watchful eye on Mike, who was scurrying everywhere, busy in every roadside clump. Now and then Pat turned to see that we were still coming, but only with polite interest. "Mike," Barbara went on, "is somewhat raffish and very much the small boy. A headstrong youngster without Pat's character or upbringing. Pat worries about him. I wonder why."

I wondered too, and I still do.

Both dogs were perfectly housebroken, but Pat had manners and Mike didn't. Pat knew from the start that the dining room was off bounds, that the kitchen was to be used only as a passageway to the backdoor, and that the couch and chairs belonged to us, not to him. Mike had to be told those things, and sometimes the telling had to be emphasized with a rolled-up newspaper.

The rolled-up newspaper was nothing new to either of the dogs. They had been disciplined that way before. They respected it and obeyed it, but they weren't afraid of it. Pat, however, had known brooms and mops, apparently had painful acquaintance with them. If Barbara or I picked up a broom, Pat cowered or ran. Mike merely scuttled out of range and waited.

We soon learned this difference between them, this fear of Pat's when either of us picked up a broom, and Barbara said, "He and Mike didn't come from the same house. Pat must have known some woman who chased him with a broom. Some spick-and-span housewife who didn't want him around."

"Or some maid," I said. "I've got a hunch he grew up with someone who had several dogs, a place with a private kennel and a big house and hired help. He was allowed in the house only when the man who owned him was there."

"Could be," she said. "He's a man's dog. No doubt about that. But Mike has had the run of the house, somewhere."

My theory seemed to be bolstered by the fact that Pat wasn't afraid of a walking stick or any outdoor tool, spade, rake or anything with a handle like a broom.

But we never found an answer, even for ourselves, to the question of Pat's worry about Mike, his deep-seated sense of responsibility for Mike's conduct. When Mike was scolded, Pat winced. One day I clouted Mike off a forbidden chair and Pat, lying in front of the fire, yelped as though I had slapped him. Mike didn't make a sound. He merely scurried out of reach and looked insulted.

But in most matters Pat seemed to make the decisions and Mike generally followed his lead. Pat chose the Navaho rug in front of the fire as their downstairs station. The first time they came upstairs Pat chose another Navaho rug at the head of the stairs as their place up there. Later Pat came to prefer my study as his upstairs retreat; but that wasn't until he and I had decided that we were more than passing acquaintances.

Mike had to explore the whole house before he accepted the fact that he had to stay out of certain rooms. But over the years I never knew Pat to go into Barbara's study, just across the hallway from mine. He never went into the guest room. And the only times he went into our bedroom were when one of us was sick abed. Then he would come to the door tentatively, almost apologetic, to see what he had sensed was wrong. He would come in, wag his tail uneasily, look his sympathy, then quietly return to the rug at the head of the stairs to await the doctor's arrival.

For one thing, though, I blessed Mike: He liked Barbara. When the dogs came in from a prowl in the pastures he went to her, all wriggles and delight, demanding attention and offering affection. When she occasionally went for a walk alone, Mike barked his delight and started off, frisking beside her. He always deserted her after the first hundred yards or so, to explore the fields, but somehow he managed to get home when she did, to bark a welcome and come in the house with her. It was warm inside. Besides, she usually rewarded him for going along by giving him a puppy biscuit when she got back.

I knew what Mike was up to, but I wondered if she did. Then one day she said, "Mike doesn't miss any bets." She laughed. "I know he's a little schemer. But a charming one. And he knows that no woman can resist attention and at least the gestures of affection. You notice that he doesn't waste much affection on you. You never give him puppy biscuits!"

We made our adjustments, all of us, and our gradual compromises. Whether we intended it or not, the dogs became a part of the household. But we spoke of them as "the dogs," not "our dogs," and each morning when I let them out and gave them their breakfast snack and watched them take off across the pasture I bade them a silent good-bye. This, I knew, might be the day when they wouldn't come back. And when we discussed them we always ended by saying, "Well, whatever happens, it's been good knowing them. We'll miss them, but they really aren't our dogs."

But, day after day, they roamed the pastures and the mountainsides and came back.

Our mountainside—it is called Tom's Hill locally, but on the older maps it is Tom's Mountain—is a rather steep, rocky slope with a thick stand of second-growth timber, a scattering of oak and maple and hickory, a good deal of birch and ash, with pine and hemlock on the higher shoulders. The mountain rises abruptly from the far side of the pastures, which are the grassy flatland that once was the river's narrow flood plain. Several springs feed brooks that flow down the mountain. The biggest spring of all feeds the springhouse from which water is piped a quarter of a mile to the house.

Above the springs the mountain rises in a series of eroding ledges, old rock that was stripped clean by glaciers of the last ice age. Over the centuries enough soil has been built up to support brushy growth and a sparse stand of trees on the ledges. At the foot of each ledge is a jumble of weathered rock, pried loose by frost and ice. At the top of the mountain the backbone of the whole ridge lies bare, tough gray granite and gneiss that the lichens, the frost and the persistent roots of determined bushes are constantly trying to tear apart.

When the first white settlers came here, in the 1730s, there was a Mohican Indian village just down the valley from our house. The Indians grew corn in the valley and hunted game on the ridges, deer, elk, panthers, bobcats, raccoons, foxes, rabbits. The white settlers also farmed the valley land and hunted the ridges and fished the river. In time, they cut much of the virgin timber on the hills, some for lumber, some for firewood, some to make charcoal for the iron furnaces of early Salisbury and Amesville. In the cutting they opened hillside fields. Some of those fields were tilled as recently as twenty or thirty years ago.

During the energetic farming period the elk vanished, the panthers were killed off and the deer retreated to the more rugged hills to the north and west. But eventually the upland fields were farmed out and the farmers retreated to the more fertile valley land. Second-growth timber grew on the ridges again and the deer came back, the deer, the bobcats, the raccoons and the foxes. The rabbits had never gone away. Rabbits persist even in the weedy back lots of a city's fringes.

By the time we came here, Tom's Mountain and the whole ridge knew the bark of the foxes again, and the cry of the bobcats. A herd of deer wintered there among the hemlocks and came down in summer dusk to graze the far edge of the pastures and in the crisp fall dawn to eat windfall apples in the orchard.

Charley talked about the foxes he had trapped on the ridge only a few years before. A telephone man who came to install a dial phone stayed to tell about hunting coons up there. And Morris, of the eager boyish heart and laughter, talked about the grouse and the bobcats as well as the coons and foxes.

Morris works for the power company, but he has roamed these hills, hunting and fishing, since he was a small boy thirty years ago. His eyes glow and his voice is eloquent as he talks of the woods and the waters and imitates the whirr of a grouse, the bark of a fox, the snarl of a bobcat. He keeps foxhounds. "My dogs," he said, "lost a fox up there on the ridge last fall and put up a bobcat. Ran him all over the hillside, and I was afraid they would corner him in the rocks and get clawed to ribbons. But he wouldn't corner and he wouldn't tree. There are several families of cats up there, but this one was the real grandpappy. When you go up there, keep an eye out for him. He's something to see." He turned to our two dogs. "I've heard that black and white hound running rabbits up there. He looks like a good hound. You'll have to hunt him, come next fall."

Everybody in the valley had heard the dogs, who had begun to run the mountainside every morning. Their voices echoed every day in the chill January air. Pat had a baritone voice that would please any hound man. Mike's voice was higher and tended to become a series of shrill, excited yaps. I soon learned to follow them, by ear, all over the mountainside. And one mild day I went part way up the hillside to listen to their music and watch them run. Before I came back to the house they had brought two rabbits past where I stood.

I came back across the home pasture and saw Charley waiting for me at the barway, waiting and listening to the dogs. When I joined him he said, "It sounds like you've got that rabbit dog."

"Two of them," I said.

Charley shook his head. "Just one. That black pup's not worth a hoot. All noise and no sense." He listened and smiled. "But that Pat hound is all right. Next fall we'll take him out and have some fun."

I wondered if Pat would still be here next fall. I began to hope he would.

The mild spell continued through the last few days of January. But February came in with a sharp change. The temperature dropped to eight above zero and I thought the dogs would be ready to stay at home. Pat would have, but Black Mike gulped his breakfast snack and headed for the mountainside. Pat hesitated, then followed. Ten minutes later I heard them, Mike's shrill yelping and Pat's deep voice, on a rabbit trail, and I thought: That's one way to keep warm.

I came in and worked at my typewriter all morning. From time to time I heard the dogs, far up the mountain, and wondered why they were out so long. Then, just before noon, I heard them a long way off, up among the ledges. Mike's high-pitched voice was almost frantic with excitement and even Pat's deep voice was full of urgency. I opened a window and listened. There were a few yelps of pain or anger, I couldn't tell which. Mike's voice shrilled. Then there was silence.

I went downstairs. Barbara was getting the noonday meal. She too had heard the dogs, and she asked, "What's happening up there on the mountain?"

"I don't know," I said. "The dogs seem to have tied into something. If they're not back in another hour or so I'll try to get up there and see what's going on."

"You don't suppose they are hurt, do you?"

"Look," I said, "they've been up there, day after day, running rabbits. They probably know more about that mountainside right now than I'll know in years. And they should know how to take care of themselves. I'm not going to worry about those two dogs. They're not even ours!"

She looked at me with a smile and said nothing. But all through dinner we kept listening. We didn't hear a sound except the wind in the trees.

It was almost one-thirty and I was just getting into my heavy coat when Barbara called from the kitchen, "Here they come!"

I went to the window. There they were, coming across the pasture. Mike was in the lead. Pat was limping and his head was down. He would come a little way, stop, rest, come on again.

"Pat's hurt!" Barbara exclaimed.

I went outdoors. Mike bounced around the woodshed, frisked past me, then turned to look back. There wasn't a mark on him. Then Pat appeared, walking slowly, painfully. His head and shoulders were caked with blood.

Pat looked up and saw me and tried to wag his tail, almost apologetic. I saw a long gash across his muzzle. His left ear was slit. The white of his chest and left shoulder was dark with dried blood. No telling what wounds he had beneath that blood.

Mike bounced up the steps and into the house. Pat came up painfully, step by step, and into the kitchen. He lay down on the linoleum floor, heaved a deep sigh and began licking his left foreleg. It had the only wound he could reach with his tongue.

Barbara brought warm water and clean cloths. I washed the blood from his head and neck. The gash across his muzzle was not very deep, a long rake of a razor-sharp claw, probably, that had missed his eye by half an inch. His left leg was ripped open, painful but not serious. But his left ear had been slit more than half its length. Apparently a claw had caught that long hound-ear and slit it like a knife. It was that wound which had bloodied him the most.

I cleaned him and examined the wounds and salved them. He took it all without a whimper. The bleeding had stopped, clotted during the long, cold trip down the mountain. When I had finished, he licked my hand, got to his feet and went into the living room and lay down in front of the fire. Mike began licking the wounds.

I phoned the veterinary. He said it sounded as though they had tangled with a bobcat. "Is he pretty badly clawed up?"

I described the wounds, told him what I had done, asked if I'd better bring him over to the vet's office.

"They're not your dogs, you say?"

"No. They're a pair of strays that came and adopted us. Should that ear be given a few stitches?"

"Wouldn't do much good. Cartilage, and it won't grow back together. He'll always have a slit ear. How about the other dog?"

"He's not even scratched. He's licking Pat's wounds right now. He's licked off all the salve I put on."

"His saliva's probably better than your salve. Bring him over if you want to, but all I could do would be to clean the wounds. And you say you've already done that. The other dog will keep them clean and he should heal all right. Farm dogs are tough. If he shows signs of infection in a few days, call me. I doubt that he will."

He didn't. For two days he lay in front of the fire, eating little and sleeping most of the time. Mike licked the wounds a dozen times a day, and when I examined them they had begun to heal from beneath, as they should. Then, the third morning, Pat limped upstairs and into my study. Partly, I think, to get away from Mike. He settled down there and slept, and occasionally he yipped in his sleep, as if in pain, and his legs jerked fiercely. He would snap his jaws and waken himself and look at me sheepishly. Then he would sigh and shift his position and go back to sleep.

All dogs dream, and Pat must have had nightmares about that encounter on the mountainside. I never knew how it came out, but the following summer when I was up among the ledges I found a heap of bones and a few tufts of coarse fur the tawny color of a bobcat. Whether that was the cat Pat tangled with, I do not know, but it could have been. It was a big cat, but not the one Morris called Grandpappy. We saw Grandpappy up there two years later, still alive and snarling.

I often wondered why Pat had a fight with a bobcat when he and Mike presumably were out running rabbits. Bobcats don't attack dogs if they can avoid it. I am quite sure that Mike was the one who instigated that fight. Mike had to be into everything. He would poke his nose into any place that had an interesting odor, or into anybody's business. He probably picked up the bobcat's scent, forgot the rabbit they were trailing, and followed the cat into a corner among the rocks. Then he would have yelped for help. And Pat, with that strange sense of responsibility for Mike, would have answered the summons. Pat never dodged a fight, no matter what were the odds. Mike, who as Charley said was "all noise and no sense," yelped and danced and stayed out of reach, and Pat did the dirty work. Anyway, Mike came back unscathed. Pat came back with all the wounds of battle.

Pat was laid up for two weeks. He spent most of that time here in my study. Looking back, it seems to me that those two weeks marked the turning point in our relationship, his and mine. The change began there in the kitchen, when I cleansed his wounds and he thanked me with a few licks of his tongue. It deepened as I recognized the courage and toughness in him, and as I suppose he found some response in me, some compound of admiration and compassion. I can't define it further, but I know that enduring matters were decided between us during those convalescent days we spent together here in this small room.

After the first two or three days of acute discomfort, when he wanted only to lie in front of the fire and sleep while nature made initial repairs, he evolved a simple routine. He would eat his breakfast snack, go out in the pasture or down along the river-bank for fifteen minutes or so to sense the morning world and tend to his own affairs. Then he would return to the house. I would hear him at the door and let him in. Mike would be in the dooryard, hoping to lure Pat for a further trip afield. Mike didn't want to be let in. Pat would limp upstairs and settle down in my study. I would go to work at the typewriter.

Half an hour later Mike, not knowing what to do with himself, would demand to be let in. He would station himself at the head of the stairs, lonely and restless. I would work and Pat would sleep and dream and rouse and look at me. I would say a word or two, he would thump the floor with his tail and go back to sleep. Occasionally Mike would come in, waken Pat and lick his wounds, then go across the hall and into Barbara's study. She would order him out and he would go downstairs. Barbara would go down on some errand and I would hear her exclaim, "Mike!" and know she had caught him on a chair. The door would open, Barbara would come back to her study, and soon we would hear Mike barking at the juncos in the yard or whining at the door to be let back in.

Afternoons, when the weather was not too bitter to face, we walked, all four of us as soon as Pat's wounds began to heal. Mike would frisk all over the roadside fields. Pat would limp ahead of us, watchful of Mike but never far from us. From time to time he would wait till we caught up, then touch my hand with his cold nose and limp along beside me. Evenings, when we sat beside the fire, reading or talking or listening to music, Pat would lie at my feet.

Of such small matters are man-dog relationships evolved. I didn't talk to him, particularly, certainly showed him no special attention. And except for those small gestures—his nose in my hand now and then and his evening nap at my feet—he made no bid for my affection. But Pat never did wear his heart on his sleeve.

Then one day Barbara said, "Pat used to be The Dog Who Walks Alone. Now he wants to walk with you."

I nodded.

"He's decided that he's your dog. You know that, don't you?"

"No," I said. "It's the other way around. He seems to have decided that I'm his man."

"There's a difference, then?"

"Yes, a big difference." But I didn't try to explain.

February passed, blustery and raw, and Pat's wounds healed. He still walked with a limp, but it was diminishing. His left ear was and always would be a mitten ear, with that long slit. The gash across his muzzle healed with scarcely any scar. He still came to my study for a morning nap, but by mid-morning he wanted out. He and Mike began to prowl the fields again and I heard their voices echoing from the lower mountainside.

March brought snow and deeper cold. The river was frozen over again, bank to bank. A late spring, Charley said. The snow piled up, a foot, then eighteen inches, and the cold held it.

Mike didn't like snow. When I let them out in the morning Mike would wrinkle his black nose in annoyance and scurry up the path to the house, eager to get in and away from that unpleasant white stuff. Pat loved snow. He would stand nosing the morning air for a moment, then take a few steps and literally dive into a snowdrift. He would roll and wallow, almost ecstatic, and leap to his feet glistening from black nose to white tail-tip with gleaming crystals. He would shake himself and look at me as much as to say, "Wonderful!"

But not even Pat could prowl the fields in the deep snow. He would trot down the shallow canyon that was the plowed-out road, puffing steamy breath and investigating the state of this glistening world. He would be gone for an hour or so, checking on all the night visitors, marking all the canine sign posts, visiting all the familiar roadside places. Then he would come back and spend most of the day in my study or in front of the fire.

Finally March blew toward its end. I saw a notice in the local newspaper that April first was the deadline for licensing dogs. On the last day of March I drove down to the town clerk's office in the village.

The clerk asked questions. I said I would have to guess at most of the answers. She said she guessed that would have to do. So we set down the required data. "Mike, black setter, aged one year . . . Pat, black and white foxhound, aged four years." Mike did look vaguely like a runty setter pup. Pat probably had fox-hound blood. Their ages could have been those I guessed. It didn't seem to matter. The clerk gave me two brass tags and I went to the hardware store and bought two leather collars.

I came home and put the tags on the collars and buckled them on the dogs. Every time they moved about the house those tags jingled, reminding us that we now were a household of four. We owned two dogs. I had said so publicly, legally.

CHAPTER 3

THE SIMPLEST way to take a dog census in any rural area is to get a dog or two of your own. Dogs are like boys. If a new boy, or a new dog, moves into a neighborhood they all make excuses to come around and see what he looks like, whether he will take an insult or resent it, whether he will fight or turn and run. They have to know. The newcomer must prove himself.

But most of the dogs here in the valley stayed close to home during the winter and the deep snow. The first one to come was Teddy, and he didn't come until a raw April day when Albert and his helper drove up in the big truck for a load of the hay Albert had stored in my big barn.

Teddy was a big, very woolly old sheep dog with a querulous bass voice. I saw him down at Albert's when we first came here to live, usually snoozing in the sun. Whenever I stopped to talk, Teddy barked furiously and came to nose me, his tail wagging. I never took Teddy seriously. If he made too much noise, Albert would say patiently, "Teddy, go lie down and be quiet." And Teddy would lumber off after Albert had shouted at him a time or two. Teddy was half deaf, Albert explained, and he was so old he had a film of cataract over both eyes. "Used to be quite a fighter," Albert said, and his tattered old ears showed it. "But he hasn't got a tooth in his head any more. He was my father's dog."

This day Teddy came up with Albert in the truck. Pat and Mike were outdoors and I soon heard Mike's shrill voice yelping insults. I decided to go down and see what was going on. I hadn't seen Albert in a couple of weeks. The dogs were making so much noise I couldn't work, anyway. Old Teddy, too, had begun to woof.

Albert was in the mow, passing bales down to his helper on the truck. He saw me and shouted a greeting and went back into the mow for another bale. All three dogs were stiff-legging it about the barnyard, old Teddy grumbling deep in his throat, Mike yapping indignantly at Teddy and getting no attention at all, Pat scratching dead grass with his hind paws, that he-dog gesture of defiant masculinity.

I don't know whether my presence touched things off or not. Dogs sometimes seem to start a rumpus just to show their owners that they have red blood in their veins. Pat had bristled over to old Teddy and they were nosing each other and rumbling mutual insults. Then, for no reason at all, Mike rushed in and leaped at Teddy. Teddy woofed at him and Mike scurried away. Looking for Mike, half-blind Teddy saw Pat and lunged at him. Down they went in a noisy uproar.

Teddy was big enough to make two of Pat, but Pat scrambled to his feet and plunged in, jaws snapping. He couldn't get a tooth-hold in Teddy's thick fur and toothless Teddy couldn't get a hold on Pat, but they made lots of noise. In the confusion, Mike sneaked in and grabbed one of Teddy's hind legs with his sharp little teeth. Teddy bellowed and Mike dodged away again.

Teddy seemed to think Pat had done it. He tried to grab Pat by the neck and shake him, but all he did was gum him and slobber him up.

Albert shouted, "Teddy, you old fool!" and began to laugh. But he jumped down onto the truck and on down to the ground. He and I began slapping the dogs apart with our leather gloves. We finally put an end to it and Albert straightened up with a grin. "Those two," he said, "could wallow all day and nobody'd really get hurt. But they make so much noise you'd think they were chewing each other's ears off, now wouldn't you?"

Pat and Teddy still rumbled threats but neither seemed to mind having the fight interrupted. Albert climbed back into the mow and Pat and Teddy were almost agreed on a truce when Mike crept back. He was all waggles of friendship, but I didn't like the look in his eye. I tried to intercept him but he snarled and leaped at Teddy again. I slapped him across the muzzle with a glove and he yelped and scurried toward the house. Teddy rumbled and glared, but Pat wasn't in the range of his dim eyesight. Nothing happened.

I waited a few minutes more. Pat and Teddy made their peace and went off together to explore the little upper pasture and I came back to the house. Mike was sulking on the front porch. I brought him inside and kept him there until Albert had finished his load and started for home, Teddy lumbering happily and noisily beside the truck. Pat went along down to the first bend in the road, then came swaggering home and sat on the front steps, apparently satisfied that he had told Teddy who was really the boss around this place.

As far as I know, Pat and Teddy never had another row. Teddy came up with Albert from time to time, and Mike yapped at him, but Teddy paid him little attention. Teddy might be half deaf and almost blind, but he was a wise old dog. He and Pat had a lasting truce, and he knew that Mike was just a noisy nuisance.

There were only two other big dogs in the valley, really big. One was a collie, a beautiful sable and a blooded dog. A man down the road, not a farmer but a professional man who worked in a nearby village, had bought him as a playmate for his children. As I heard the story, the collie was an ideal companion for the children for a year or two. Then something happened, nobody seemed to know just what. The collie just walked off and left the children. He went to a farm a mile or so away and announced that he was going to live there. The owner took him home a dozen times, pampered him, petted him, made a great fuss over him. The collie accepted it all with typical collie dignity, but after a day or two of lavish meals and high living he always went back to the farmhouse where he got scraps and a minimum of attention. Finally his owner gave up and stopped trying to lure him back.

Now and then I saw this collie on my way to the village. If it was morning, he would be out with the farmer trailing the cows down the road to a pasture. He herded those cows with a sure instinct, nipping a laggard's heels, barking softly when necessary, urging them past the wrong gate and into the right one. Then, the cows pastured and the barway closed, he walked back to the barnyard with the farmer, asking neither praise nor attention. If it was evening, he brought the cows from pasture to barn with the same sure instinct and quiet patience, urging the dawdlers, gently checking the galloping calves, firmly turning back the wanderers.

I once asked the farmer if he had trained the collie to this job. He gave me a slow smile and a shake of his head. "The dog just likes cows, I guess. Collies are that way. I never trained him. He just knew."

The farmer had two dogs of his own, just country dogs. They played with his children but were no help with the cows or anything else. The collie tolerated the other dogs, sometimes lay in the sun with them, but he never seemed to play with the farmer's children. Maybe he went up there to get away from children, and to be near cows.

Once in a while this collie came up the road as far as our place. He always came alone. He was that kind of dog, a loner. The first time he came, Mike dashed down the road, yelping furiously. Pat followed at a little distance, barking his ownership bark. Mike strutted up to the collie and yelped all kinds of epithets, and the collie turned his head and gave Mike one look and didn't break his stride. Mike shut up, like that, as though awed, and went to the other side of the road and trotted along, keeping pace with the collie but quiet, for a change.

Pat came along and the collie paused and looked at him. Pat went up to him and they smelled each other. Pat bristled and the collie looked down his long, slim nose at him once or twice and trotted on up the road. He didn't stop at Pat's marking places and he didn't go nosing along the roadside. He just kept trotting with the quiet, confident air of a casual passer-by, not an invader or a challenger. And Pat stood and watched.

Then Pat loped back to his own yard, Mike at his heels, and they sat and watched as the collie trotted past, sedate and minding his own business. Ten minutes later the collie came back down the road, his visit up here ended. Mike dashed at him, yelping, and got the same cool, distant treatment as before, and gave up. Pat didn't even get up from the grass.

The collie came up this way only a few times, and always the same thing happened. Pat barked announcement of his coming, went down the road a little way, and they exchanged dignified greetings. Then Pat came back to his own yard and made no more fuss. Mike, however, was both furious and frustrated. The collie wouldn't talk back, wouldn't even acknowledge his existence by growling at him.

The other big dog, really big, was a black Newfoundland, all black, not even one white paw. He was almost as big as a bear and twice as deliberate. In fact, he was mistaken for a bear a couple of times by outlanders, and when a black bear actually visited the valley a few years later the reports of his presence were laughed at by a good many people who were sure it was just the old Newfoundland ambling along a back road at dusk. The bear never stopped in here and I never saw him, but he was properly identified as a bear. And a day or two later he vanished from this area and was seen on the other side of the ridge, then ten miles away. He was traveling somewhere, apparently, and kept on going.

The Newfoundland also lived some distance down the valley and usually stayed close to home. But one day he wandered up this far. Pat saw him first and went down the road to meet him, barking madly. Mike had been chasing birds, or some such nonsense, but when he heard Pat he, too, went tearing down the road.

Pat reached the Newfoundland first, circled him cautiously, and the Newfoundland stared at him and wagged his long tail. Pat went up to him and tried to nose him and the Newfoundland thrust out a tongue big as a veal tongue and slobbered Pat's face. Pat sneezed and went to the roadside and kicked grass and came back and strutted on tiptoe, looking like a pigmy beside the big fellow. He could almost have walked beneath the Newfoundland's belly and never touched a hair. The big dog grinned at him and trotted up the road like a sway-backed plow horse.

Then Mike arrived, ears flying, yelling like a hellion. The Newfoundland looked at him as though in amusement and Mike braked to a stop. I think he was astonished that this really was a dog. He probably had never seen so much dog in one skin. He crept forward cautiously and strained up to sniff the Newfoundland's nose, then jerked back and barked. The Newfoundland sat down ponderously and opened his huge mouth and panted. Mike just stared. Then he yelped and danced around, looking at the Newfoundland from all angles. He apparently decided that this was a dog, after all, and cavorted playfully. To my astonishment, the Newfoundland wanted to play too. He also cavorted, and it was like a circus elephant dancing.

They romped up the road and Pat came on home, looking back now and then as though disgusted. Mike dashed between the Newfoundland's legs and yipped happily, and the Newfoundland loped about, chasing him, until he was tired out. Then they went over to the riverbank and lay down in the grass, a mountain of black fur and a molehill of black fur, and the Newfoundland stared at Mike like a long-eared Bert Lahr.

Finally the Newfoundland got to his feet and started back home. Mike cavorted beside him down to the bend of the road. But playtime was over. The Newfoundland probably remembered that it was time for his five pounds of noonday meat. He padded down the road and Mike came home. He lay in the yard all afternoon, looking wistfully down the road as though wishing he could go to the circus all over again.

The Newfoundland never came back, and as far as I know Mike never went down to see him. Maybe he was content to let it be a dream, a fantastic experience that never could have really happened.

The other dogs were just dogs, as far as Pat and Mike were

concerned. They didn't matter either way. The sleek-haired black one and the uncombed yellow one came and looked and were chased and didn't come back. There was a row or two, mostly noise and nobody hurt. And there was a rat-tailed yellow one that came past one afternoon, from I don't know where. He was nondescript looking, a cur-dog type. And he was a curious creature, stopping at all the marking places and nosing into all the roadside bushes. Pat resented that. Pat barked a time or two and Mike yelped, and they set off down the road, truculent as could be. The stranger took one look, then turned and trotted away. Pat took after him. I thought Pat was going to catch him and fur would really fly. Pat could run pretty fast. But as he began to close in on the yellow dog the stranger took off. He ran like a whippet. He made Pat look like a third-rater. Pat chased him a hundred yards and lost ground at every jump, and Pat just stopped and stared. That ungainly-looking dog could have outrun a fox.

One afternoon a beagle pup came wandering up the road. He was obviously a stranger and lost. He couldn't have been more than six months old and was still all big paws and long ears and good nature. The dogs barked and charged out to challenge him, and he wagged his tail and woofed happily, as though welcoming canine company in this strange, alien world. He took all the gruffness out of them in an instant. They came back up the road, a congenial trio, and within five minutes Mike was like a country cousin showing the city boy all his special tricks and treasures.

Pat watched them like an indulgent uncle until they began digging in the edge of the flower garden. He hurried over and growled them away and lay down to guard the place. Not, I am sure, because he knew it was a flower garden. He hadn't yet learned that. He probably had a bone buried there and wasn't going to let two happy-go-lucky kids appropriate it.

Mike and the brown and white pup romped away and rolled in the grass and chewed each other's ears and chased each other's tails. Mike found a spruce cone and tossed it in the air and chased it and waited for the beagle to try to take it away from him. The pup didn't know that game, and Mike wasn't much of a teacher. He forgot the cone and led a race out to the barn. They played there for a while, then a haphazard game of tag took them into the middle pasture. The pup, with his beagle nose, found a rabbit scent, yelped shrilly and bounded off on the trail. Mike went along. They were gone almost two hours, yipping the lower mountainside. Then they came home, worn out, and lay in the sun and napped.

Finally a top-down convertible came cruising up the road, very slowly. Pat announced that it had stopped here and I went to the door. A youngish man in brand new khakis came up the walk. Mike and the pup had been wakened by Pat's barking and came around the house to share the excitement. The man saw the pup and exclaimed, "Leslie!"

The pup ran to him, one big waggle, and the man picked him up in his arms. The pup squirmed with pleasure and licked the man's face and the man laughed and said to me, "I've been looking for this little guy for three hours. Thanks for taking him in."

We talked a few minutes. The man was from a city forty miles from here. A girl friend had given the pup to him a month ago and he had named him after her, since the name seemed to be not strictly feminine. "It seemed a nice day to let him get a sniff of the country, so I drove over this way. Let him out of the car a couple of miles down the road to romp a bit, and he took off after a rabbit and didn't come back." He laughed. "I didn't think he was old enough to know what a rabbit smelled like, but I guess it's born in them."

He looked around. "You've got a beautiful place here. But it must be lonely. Not another house in sight!"

I wished I could explain loneliness to him, the loneliness that can break a man's heart in the midst of a crowd. But he was young. He would have to learn about such things himself, the way we learn all the really difficult lessons. But I did smile at his saying this place was beautiful. The house is just an old farmhouse, architecturally stark. Maybe he meant the mountainside, though, and the river. And the contrast with the city.

"We like it," I said. And he went back to his car, put the pup on the seat beside him and drove back the way he had come. Mike stood and looked after them for a long time. Mike hadn't had such a carefree playmate in months, if ever. I think Mike would have happily gone along, if invited. When he finally turned away and went and lay down beside Pat he looked at him as though saying, "It isn't that I don't like you, Uncle Pat. But I wish you were a puppy, once in a while. You really think life is awfully serious."

The most challenging dogs were those who ran the tangled woods across the river. Pat and Mike resented them. So did we, especially when they yelped and yowled and bellowed in the night, as they sometimes did.

The woods over there are brushy second growth, ideal cover for deer and rabbits and grouse. I knew little about those woods at the time, but during the fall I had heard hunters banging away over there and heard their dogs almost every day. They were after rabbits, but now and then the dogs got out of hand.

One afternoon there was a particularly loud uproar, several hounds in on it. I went out on the porch to watch and listen. For a time I heard two men, far off, shouting at the dogs, trying to call them in, but the dogs paid no attention. The chase continued, loud and excited. Then there was a crashing in the brush directly across the river and a chorus of dogs just beyond. Suddenly a big doe came through the brush, looked back, and lunged down the bank and into the water. She swam toward our shore, low in the water and obviously tired. She had swum only about thirty feet when three big hounds burst from the brush and saw her and howled in frustration. The doe looked back and swam faster. The dogs charged up and down the muddy bank, but none of them went into the water after her.

She swam on across, hauled herself wearily ashore just below my dock, came up the bank and stood at the edge of the road, quivering and breathing hard. She looked back, at the dogs still yelping the far riverbank. She was directly in front of the house and I was in plain sight, not a hundred feet from her. But she showed no fear of me if, indeed, she even saw me. She had escaped the dogs. What greater danger could I present? She caught her breath, then walked up the road past my garage, crawled through the wire fence and walked slowly across the upper pasture. She was too tired to leap the fence, or the one beyond. She crawled through the second fence and vanished in the brush on the mountainside. The dogs had run her hard and a long way.

The dogs that ran her weren't a pack of wild dogs. They were probably rabbit dogs, not particularly well trained. They had put up this doe, one of them had taken after her and the others had joined in the excitement of the chase. Some hunters are careless and lax in discipline, apparently not knowing, or not caring, that when a dog starts chasing deer that dog will soon become a worthless hound, one that will chase anything in the woods.

We've never had a pack of wild dogs in the valley that I know of. Some rural areas do have them, and they are death not only on deer but on calves and sheep. They are worse than wolves because they can go unrecognized for weeks. Then they have to be hunted down, and they are usually crafty as well as vicious. A few years later three or four strange hounds ran the ridge together for a short time, and we thought we would have to take high-caliber measures. But that was later.

There was no hunting, of course, that first spring after Pat and Mike came here. But stray dogs, or wandering dogs, ran the woods across the river every few days. And on an occasional night. Our dogs resented them, noisily.

There was one with a booming voice and I thought, hearing him, that he must be a regular mastiff of a dog. One April day he was roaring away over there, coming closer and closer to the river, and both Pat and Mike went down to the riverbank and barked challenge. I went out to watch, hoping to get a look, at last, at this behemoth of a dog. The deep bellow echoed all across the valley and Mike became especially frantic, dashing right down to the water's edge. But never wetting his feet. Mike hated the water. Pat stayed up on the bank, bristling, barking a warning from time to time.

Finally a short-legged brown hound not much bigger than Mike came out of the brush and down to the water's edge on the far side. I waited for the big dog to appear. And this little brown fellow sniffed and looked around and began to bellow. I couldn't believe it. He had a voice like a basso profundo. I began to laugh. Pat barked a time or two, just his way of saying, "Don't come over here or there'll be trouble. I own this place." Mike yelped, but not with real conviction.

The little brown hound bellowed another time or two, lapped

39

a few mouthfuls of water and went back into the brush. Every time after that when I heard that deep, echoing bellow I had to smile. Such a big voice for such a small dog. If he had been a foxhound, I know men who would have bid high for him, just to hear that voice on a fox trail in November.

I never heard him after those few weeks in April. Maybe some foxhunter heard him and got hold of him and taught him the things any dog with a voice like that should be taught.

Inevitably, there was the counterpart for that big-voiced little hound. There was the brown and white hound, bigger than a setter, who had a hysterical soprano voice. He was even more shrill than Mike at his shrillest. He prowled those woods, baying like a banshee, for days. Chasing rabbits, apparently, for I never heard the crashing of brush ahead of him that meant a deer in flight. I especially resented him at night, and he was also a night-runner. That voice of his was hair-raising to one wakened from sleep, for he achieved a sound, at least in the moonless darkness, that was like the scream of a frightened child.

Those dogs never crossed the river. I doubt that it was because of Pat's warning, or Mike's. Their warnings were more or less routine. Pat's were, at least. I sometimes thought Mike yelped just to hear the echo of his own voice, and sometimes I am sure he yowled to get an answer. But I never saw one of those dogs cross the railroad trestle just up the road or swim the river.

I mentioned this to Charley one day. "Good thing they don't," he said. "If they came over here and started to run the deer, we'd have to do something." Then he grinned. "If you think they're noisy you should have been here a few years back. We used to have quite a few coon dogs, and some pretty good fox dogs, too. We kept them at home daytimes and we didn't let them run at night unless we went out with them. But when we took them out there was a lot of dog music. You got here too late to know what this valley can sound like with the coon dogs really running in the moonlight."

Then he looked at Pat and Mike. "Those two," he said, "can give you some idea, when they get going after a rabbit. Sometimes when I come past I just have to stop the truck and listen. To that Pat dog especially. But that black one—" He shook his head. I knew what he meant. I knew what Charley thought of

Mike. And as the weeks passed I found that I couldn't honestly challenge Charley's judgment.

CHAPTER 4

I AM CONVINCED that some dogs, like some people, are corrupted by prosperity. I don't know why, but perhaps it involves some quality in the moral fiber. It could be, of course, that we expected too much of Mike, more maturity and more stability or perhaps more adaptability than was his inherited lot. We and our ways were baffling to Mike, and his ways became more and more annoying to us.

When we had friends in for an evening, Mike charmed everyone for the first five minutes. He was cute. He was friendly. His black coat glistened, his eyes sparkled, he was full of life and friendliness. Pat, lying quietly in front of the fire, polite but reserved, got few second looks. Pat tolerated guests, but he never solicited or appreciated their attention. People glanced at him, said, "What a nice, quiet dog," and turned to rub Mike's long, silky ears. But five minutes of attention were never enough for Mike. Ignored, he licked hands, rubbed ankles, tried to climb into laps, until he was ordered out of the room.

We tried to excuse him, both of us, saying he was just a pup. Even the evening when he snatched a sandwich from a plate on the coffee table earned him only a slap and a night's disgrace. But when he sneaked into the kitchen and stole a hamburger patty from the table he got a trouncing. He had been fed less than an hour before and he hadn't finished his own meal.

Barbara exclaimed, "Mike, you are a thief!" And he was banished from the house for two days. Pat, with that strange streak of responsibility, insisted on banishment with him and wouldn't come inside until Mike was admitted again.

Mike did have a sense of play that was missing in Pat. He loved a ball and would chase one as long as I wanted to toss it for him. And never was it mere ball-chasing. Show-off that he was, Mike made a performance of it, tossing the ball, somersaulting over it, growling at it, sometimes tossing it in the air and chasing it all by himself. Perhaps I could have taught him to do tricks, for he was undoubtedly both clever and intelligent; but dog tricks never appealed to me. I would rather have my dog a dog, not a clown or an acrobat.

Mike loved all moving things. I have seen him stand and bark at a waving tree branch with one winter leaf still clinging to it. Not merely a bark, but a delighted bark. And he chased birds, not to catch them but to see them fly. All winter long he would sneak around the house and dash into a flock of unsuspecting juncos, then stand barking in sheer excitement as they scattered in the air. One early spring day I saw him standing in the yard, staring up and barking madly. I went out to see the cause of his excitement, and there was a red-tail hawk slowly circling just above the treetops. And when the first ducks arrived Mike spent hours on the riverbank. He would lie in the grass, waiting for the ducks to swim in toward the bank, then leap to his feet, bark, and watch entranced as they beat the water to a froth in their alarmed take-off.

Pat watched all such cavorting with a solemn look of detachment. I wouldn't say he disapproved. He just wasn't interested. Such capers, he seemed to be saying, were for children. I tried a few times to interest him in a ball or a thrown stick, but he gave me a look that said quite plainly, "If you want it, why did you throw it away? Go chase it yourself." He made me feel so sheepish that I gave up such nonsense with Pat.

Both dogs liked children, though in quite different ways. Mike regarded them as fellow juveniles who would play tag, chase balls, frighten birds and romp all over the place. Pat regarded them as small, friendly persons to be watched over, protected and indulged. Perhaps it was a part of his protective nature, that strange sense of responsibility. A two-year-old could wallow him, pull his ears and tail, literally walk all over him, and the most he ever did was get up and walk away. Mike would yelp and sometimes nip at such treatment. Pat never, to my knowledge, nipped or snapped at a child.

But Pat wasn't really a house dog. He was an outdoor dog, and the pastures, the fields and the mountainside were his chosen province. Morning after morning he politely suggested that I go with him to explore that wonderful world. If I went, he investigated every grass clump and brush patch until he put up a rabbit. Then he was in his element. Once a rabbit was up, he uttered a quick series of announcement yelps and lined out on the trail, baying his course. I learned to know by his voice whether he was quartering for a lost scent, hot on the trail, or announcing that the rabbit had run into a hole and quit the game.

Mike, who always went along, made all the gestures, but whereas Pat was a professional, Mike was still an amateur. When a rabbit was put up, Mike yelped in ecstatic frenzy. On the trail he was shrill and continually excited. If a rabbit ran in, Mike often howled in juvenile frustration. And sometimes, even on a hot scent, Mike would stop to bark at a blue jay or a gray squirrel.

I was almost as much of an amateur as Mike, though I grew up hunting rabbits. But in the West we used dogs only to run the far-ranging jack rabbits on the plains. Cottontails, in that grassy, brush-free land, seldom ventured far from their holes, so we hunted them without dogs and snap-shot at them on sight. But the cottontails here in this brushy hill country were a different breed with different habits.

My friend Morris tried to explain it to me. "These rabbits," he said, "run in circles like your western jacks, but smaller circles. And a good rabbit dog, our kind of dog, trails by scent, never by sight. All we want a dog to do is keep the rabbit moving, and he will circle back to where the dog jumped him. You can tell by your dog's voice where he is and what's going on. You take a stand near the place the dog puts him up and wait, and the dog brings him back past you. If the rabbit doesn't run in. If he does run in, the dog tells you."

Morris explained, and Pat demonstrated. When I went up on the mountain with him—and Mike; Mike always went along—Pat put up a rabbit, kept him going, told me by his voice just what was happening, and eventually brought the rabbit back past where I was waiting. Since I didn't take a gun, it being off-season for rabbits, sometimes the dogs brought the same rabbit past me twice. And always Pat was so intent on the trail that he paid no attention to me. Mike, open to any distraction, always saw me and came frisking up, panting, waggling and begging for praise. Whether I praised him or not, he was soon off again, on Pat's trail, or the rabbit's, or to chase a bird or a squirrel.

But I had work to do. I couldn't spend all my time up there on the mountainside. I came back to my typewriter, and the dogs went alone. They spent almost every morning keeping the mountainside's rabbits on the jump and making the valley echo. But by noon they were home again, properly tired, and spent the afternoons dozing in the sun in the dooryard while Barbara and I, as spring slowly advanced, got air and exercise in the garden.

One sunny afternoon the last week in April a pickup truck stopped out front and a little man in dungarees got out and came over to where I was pulling quack grass out of the flower garden. The dogs leaped up and barked and he smiled at them and gave them an appraising look before he greeted me. It was Dave, the dog warden. He commented on the weather and he watched a bumblebee at a yellow crocus, and he spoke of the red tips of the peonies just coming through the ground. And then he said, "I hear your dogs like government beef."

I didn't understand.

"They've been running deer," he said.

I was stunned. "Who said that?" I demanded.

"I had a report," he said. "It's fawn season, and when I get a report like that I have to do something about it." He looked at me, then looked away. Dave is one of the most kindhearted men in the world, a man who makes friends of woodchucks, foxes and squirrels. And he loves dogs. He looked at me again, and he asked, "Those are the dogs you phoned me about right after Christmas?"

"Yes."

"You advertised them?"

I nodded. "There wasn't any reply, so I licensed them. Look, Dave, they don't run deer. They just run rabbits. And they don't run rabbits anywhere except on my own land."

"Deer," Dave reminded me, "belong to the state."

"But they don't run deer!"

"I had a report that they do."

I knew perfectly well that if the report was right the dogs

44

were in trouble. Dogs running deer aren't merely a noisy nuisance; they are outlaws. Any game warden or dog warden is authorized to destroy such dogs if they are caught in the act. And dogs that kill fawns are doubly guilty. And this was fawning season.

"Are you going to take them and destroy them, Dave?" I asked.

He shook his head slowly. "Not on hearsay evidence."

"What do you want me to do?"

"Tie them up till after fawning season, at least. Maybe tying up one of them would do it. Unless he's a real killer, a dog seldom runs deer alone. Or maybe you could give one of them away."

"Do you really think these dogs are deer-killers?"

"I don't know. If I knew they were, I'd have no choice. I'd have to destroy them. It doesn't take a very big dog to kill a fawn." And he went back to his truck and got in and drove away.

Barbara was in the house. I came in and told her, and she exclaimed, "I don't believe it! They don't even kill rabbits, so why should they kill deer?"

"I don't believe it either," I said, "but we're going to have to tie one of them up."

"Who reported them?" she demanded.

"Dave wouldn't say. It doesn't matter. With all the noise they make, it could be someone on the other side of the mountain."

"And he said to tie one of them up? Why only one?"

I told her that Dave had said a dog seldom runs deer alone. And I said that Mike would be tied up tomorrow morning.

"Why Mike?"

"Mike is the one who always says, 'Let's go!' "

"This," she said, "will be something to watch."

The next morning I got a quarter-inch rope and tethered Mike to a stake in the side yard. He looked at me as though I were the most despicable of sadists, then sighed and lay down on the grass and watched me go into the house. Pat watched, then went to a sunny spot and lay down and went to sleep.

I came to my study and went to work. But little work was done that morning. First Mike began to howl. I let him howl for ten minutes, then shouted him quiet. Five minutes of silence, then he began to whine. The whines became heartbroken cries. I opened the window and shouted him to silence once more. Ten minutes of silence and Barbara shouted up the stairs, "He's trying to commit suicide!" I looked out. Mike was leaping at the end of his tether, leaping madly as though trying to break his neck. Twice he was jerked into a complete somersault. But after every two or three leaps he paused and looked at the house, hopeful.

I went downstairs and Barbara and I watched him from the window and she agreed that it was all an act. But after a few minutes Mike went to the very end of the rope, stretched out and lay down, the rope taut. He began to whimper and heave his ribs as though slowly choking to death. He almost fooled me, and he did fool Barbara. She dashed outdoors to rescue him. As soon as he saw her, Mike got to his feet, whimpered, crept to her, licked her hands and begged for freedom. She came back to the house, indignant at being so taken in.

After that there was half an hour's silence. Then Barbara shouted up to me, "He's gone! Both of them are gone!"

I went downstairs and outdoors and even before I looked at the rope I heard them yelping on the mountainside. Mike had simply cut the rope with his teeth and away they had gone.

That afternoon I went to the village and bought a five-foot dog chain. Next morning I snapped it on Mike's collar and tied the other end to the tether. Mike went through his whole routine of the day before. Then, about eleven o'clock, he was gone again. Both dogs were gone. Mike had worked his way down that chain, testing it link by link, then had cut the rope.

I went up the mountain after them. I had no trouble finding them for the dangling chain had tangled in the brush. Mike, tethered more securely than I had had him here at home, was yowling for help. Pat was lying in the sun nearby, waiting.

For the next two days I kept Mike at home by wiring the chain to the stake. But he made such a distracting uproar that I finally let him loose and tied Pat up to see what would happen. Pat was insulted, but he engaged in no melodramatics. He settled down and all was peaceful. For just about an hour. Then I heard Mike yelping the mountainside alone.

Barbara said, "I guess that settles Mike. You can't spend your time chasing him up on the mountain, and I can't spend my time guarding the food and policing the furniture."

Mike came home, looking both guilty and defiant, just after

noon, and I chained him up. Then I went to the village and put a classified ad in the weekly newspaper. "PUPPY TO GIVE AWAY. Black puppy one year old, affectionate, housebroken, needs children for company in a good home."

The first phone call was from a woman who lived ten miles away. She had two small boys. The older boy had a dog of his own and the younger boy wanted one. They had a big place and they loved dogs. I told her to come the next afternoon, with the boys, and see how they and Mike got along.

I had scarcely hung up when another call came, from a man who lived on the other side of the village. He had a six-year-old boy whose puppy had been killed by a car only a few days before. The boy was heartbroken. Please, couldn't he have this dog? I explained the situation and said I would phone him the next afternoon.

The woman arrived with her two boys. I let Mike off the chain and, with his incredible intuition, he went at once to the smaller boy and practically said, "Where have you been all my life?" Barbara had said to me only that morning that she was sure Mike knew what was up and that he would probably be an absolute darling when the people came to look at him. "Mike," she said, "is one of those people who always land on their feet." Now, as Mike and the little boy romped about the lawn, she gave me a knowing look and a meaningful smile.

But Mike, for all his sins, had a place in Barbara's heart. She asked the mother, "You have another dog, haven't you? I wonder how he and Mike will get along. After all, we want Mike to be happy."

The woman smiled. "Sandy," she said, "can get along with any dog. He never fights. He's the most good-natured dog alive."

"I wish you'd brought him," Barbara said. "Is he a big dog?"

"A collie. Collies are never quarrelsome."

"I'd like to see them together. Just to be sure. We don't want Mike to be bullied or unhappy."

I smiled to myself but kept my mouth shut. There probably were dogs somewhere who could bully Mike. This might be one.

The woman drove home and came back with Sandy. Sandy was a beautiful dog, a sable collie big as the one down the road. He got out of the car, majestic and curious but polite as only

47

collies can be. He looked around, came over and was introduced to us, and he looked with friendly curiosity at Pat, lying watchful in the sun at the edge of the yard. I had tethered Pat to keep him in the background while we settled Mike's future.

Mike had greeted the boys again with all his wriggling delight, but as soon as he saw Sandy he seemed to stiffen. I saw his tail go straight, his ears lift to a half-cock and his eyes glint. He came over to Sandy, his stiff tail wagging slowly, walking almost like a cat. I hoped Sandy would be cool and remote, as the other collie had been. Mike came up to Sandy and they touched noses. No, Sandy was doing it all wrong. He was being friendly. They sniffed. And suddenly Mike rasped, "Rrrrr-awr!" and leaped at Sandy's throat.

Sandy went back on his haunches, startled and insulted. I made a grab for Mike's collar, and missed. Sandy ran for the car, his tail between his legs, Mike snapping at his heels. The woman shouted, the boys yelled, and Sandy leaped for the open car window, missed, scratched the car frantically with his claws. Mike was yapping so excitedly that he never did really set his teeth in any part of Sandy. Then I caught up with them, grabbed Mike by the scruff of the neck, slapped him across the muzzle a time or two and hauled him away. Sandy clawed his way up and over the door to safety in the car.

I dragged Mike over to the stake and chain, but I took my time about snapping the chain to his collar. I was trying to put down my laughter. Then I heard the woman say to Barbara, "I never saw such a vicious little mongrel! Why, he could have *killed* poor old Sandy! . . . Come on, boys." And they left in a cloud of indignation.

When they were out of sight I asked, "Which dog was it you didn't want to have bullied?"

Barbara smiled, then looked at Mike. He was watching her with a hangdog expression, his tail down but wagging hopefully; and I was sure I saw the scheming look in his eyes. He knew that at that moment it wouldn't take much to make Barbara, and possibly me, change the decision about his fate. But I didn't give him a chance. I caught Barbara's hand and said, "Come on in. I have to phone that man with the little boy."

I made the phone call, and when we looked out the window a

few minutes later Mike was working his way down the chain, testing it link by link with his teeth. He sensed us watching him and dropped the chain and lay down, all injured innocence and resignation. The critical moment had passed. Mike had sealed his own sentence of banishment.

The man and the little boy arrived about five o'clock. He was a stocky little dark-haired man with smiling eyes, and the boy was a stocky little dark-haired boy with a solemn face. They got out of the car and the boy's face lit up with laughter the moment he saw Mike. I let Mike off the chain and boy and dog ran to each other and went galloping about the yard, friends immediately.

The man watched them, beaming. "Just look at those two!" he said. "Made for each other." He turned to us. "You call the pup Mike? My boy's name is Michael. Michael and Mike. Nice combination, huh?" he laughed.

We watched small boy and small dog for several minutes, and I looked at Barbara. She was smiling, satisfied.

The man said, "It looks right, doesn't it. Looks like they were made for each other."

"Yes," I said. "But I've got to be fair with you. Don't expect too much of Mike. He's not perfect."

"Who is?" The man grinned.

"Sometimes he gets on the furniture, and——"

"Our furniture is the kind it doesn't matter, just as long as he likes the boy."

"He doesn't chew rugs, but he's swiped a hamburger or two."

"Michael likes hamburgers too. They'll make a good team." Then he asked, "Is he a fighter?"

I glanced at Barbara, and she began to laugh. "You'd better tell him. He'd just as well know the worst."

So I told him about Mike and Sandy.

The man laughed till the tears came. "There's two or three mutts in my neighborhood," he said, "that are just asking for it. I don't like a quarrelsome dog, but I wouldn't have a coward on the place. I guess he can take care of himself. . . . Well, Michael, what do you say, boy? Do you like the dog?"

Michael came over to us, hauling Mike along by one of his long, silky ears. Mike yipped a time or two and gnawed at the boy's fingers. Finally he nipped too hard and the boy exclaimed in pain and slapped him, then dropped to his knees, hugged him, and they rolled in the grass. The boy looked up, pushed Mike's eager tongue away from his face, and cried, "I love him!"

"Do you want him?" the father asked.

"Yes, I want him! He's mine!"

I turned to Barbara. She said, "I guess there's not much question about it, is there?"

"Michael," I said, "you've got a dog. A dog named Mike. Take good care of him."

Michael leaped to his feet, shouted, "Whee! Whoopee! Here, Mike! Here, Mike!" And he ran to the car, Mike leaping beside him. The boy opened the car door, Mike leaped in and onto the front seat. Michael climbed in beside him and beeped the horn.

The man turned to us and shook hands. "You don't know what this means," he said. "Michael's been lost without his dog. Didn't want to eat, didn't want to play. Nothing. Now look at him!" Then he asked, "Does he chase cars?"

"No," I said. "That's one thing I can say for Mike, he doesn't chase cars."

"Thank God! I'd take him anyway and try to break him of it, but if he doesn't, that's wonderful. Maybe he'll be around for a while. . . . Well, I don't know how to thank you, but—just look at those two!"

We went with him to the car. He got behind the wheel, started the motor. Barbara shouted, "Mike! Good-bye, Mike!"

Mike turned and looked at her, then at me. Then his tongue went out and he licked Michael's ear. Michael hugged him, and Mike squirmed free and sat up and barked happily as they drove away. He didn't look back, not once.

We came back across the yard and I untied the rope from Pat's collar. He shook himself and went out to the road and sniffed where the car had been parked. He looked down the road, and then he seemed to sigh. He turned and came back across the yard to us, and he touched my hand with his nose.

I pulled up the tether stake, loosened the chain from it and tossed the stake into the woodshed. I hung up the chain and coiled the rope and put it away. I wasn't sure, but I hoped and believed I wouldn't need it again.

We came into the house, the three of us, and Pat looked around, then went to the rug in front of the Franklin stove and lay down. He lay there a moment, then looked up, as though asking if everything was all right. He came to me and nosed my hand again, and he went to Barbara. She rubbed his ears and said, "It's all right, Pat. You're going to stay." Then he went back and lay down.

At supper Barbara said, "He was a tramp and a scamp, but a lovable scamp. I'll miss him."

"Why," I asked, "do women fall for the rascal type, the romantic heel?"

"Do they?"

"You just proved it. Mike, the lovable scamp. He was a thief, a fraud, and a coward when the chips were down, as they were with the bobcat. But he was affectionate when affection would get him what he wanted. He was a little outlaw who could, when he wanted to, be a charmer. Now you call him a lovable scamp, and say you'll miss him."

"Mike," she said, "wasn't really a fraud. He just lived by a different code, that's all. When he was bad he was impossible, and when he was good he was wonderful. When he gave me his heart he gave every ounce of it, even if he took it all back five minutes later. I guess you wouldn't understand, being a man, the kind of man you are. But don't just condemn him, and don't say I fell for him just because he was a lovable little scoundrel."

Later that evening, sitting in front of the fire, she said, "I'll bet he's asleep in the best chair in the house right now."

"Full as a tick. They probably fed him right from the table."

"Undoubtedly. And he'll sleep on Michael's bed."

"Probably on Michael's pillow."

"I wonder," she said, "where he would have slept at Sandy's house."

"In Sandy's bed."

"Poor old Sandy." She laughed. "I really felt sorry for him."

"Sandy," I said, "will have nightmares, about little black dogs all over the place. He'll yip and yelp and have a terrible night."

Pat sat up and yawned. He looked around the room, puzzling, then yawned again and came over and looked at me.

"Bedtime?" I asked.

He wagged his tail and turned toward the back door.

I took him outdoors. He looked behind him, as though expecting Mike, then seemed to remember. He sniffed the air, looked across the pasture toward the mountain. Then he looked at me and went to the woodshed door. I opened it and he went inside, turned around twice and lay down. "See you in the morning, Pat," I said, and I closed the door and went back in the house.

"I do miss Mike," Barbara said. "And I think Pat does."

"I miss him too," I said. "The way I miss a headache when it stops throbbing. Maybe I can get some work done tomorrow."

"Tough guy."

"Hard as nails."

But that night I dreamed of Mike, dreamed I heard him howling. I wakened and was half out of bed before I realized that it was a dream. I lay back, and before I went to sleep again I blessed Mike and wished him well. Mike had loved Barbara, in his own way. He had given her affection, for whatever purpose, and he had taught her that dogs were people. Some dogs. I hoped that Pat, too, would love her, in time. And in Pat's own way.

CHAPTER 5

DAVE, the dog warden, was right. After we sent Mike away, Pat stayed at home. But for some time he was restless and uneasy. He would eat his breakfast snack, make a brief excursion into the home pasture or down the road, then come back and lie in the sun on the front steps or in the side yard. He would lie there, apparently napping, but from time to time he would lift his head or get to his feet and watch and listen. Barbara said he was like a mother whose only child has gone off to school for the first time. Sometimes he would go out into the road and stand and look. Then he would come back and lie down and nap once more, or he would ask to be let into the house. Inside, he would look around, stand abstracted for a few moments, then go back outside or come up here to my study. He came here more often than he had since he was recovering from his bout with the wild cat.

He missed Mike, but I doubt that he missed him as a companion so much as he missed him as a responsibility. Pat is a most responsible dog. Mike was his ward, and it made no difference whether the wardship was thrust upon him, in some strange manner, or he assumed it voluntarily. And now Mike was no longer here. There was a gap in his life and he didn't quite know what to do about it.

Afternoons, he would go for a walk with us, but on those walks he never wandered far. And he kept coming back to us, to thrust his nose into my hand as though for reassurance. And when I let him out of the woodshed in the morning he seemed so glad to see me that I wondered if he thought we might pack up and move away in the night. And before anyone exclaims that he was a victim of insecurity, I will say that Pat has always been the most inwardly secure dog I ever knew. By all the signs I could read, he was sure that he could take care of himself, no matter what happened. But he must have wondered what was going to happen. He had adopted a home, chosen to live with us. We had banished Mike, sent him away, and Mike hadn't come back. Pat could be excused for wondering what would happen next.

This went on for a week or more. Then one morning when I let him out of the woodshed and met that "Oh, you're still here" look, I told Barbara that I was going to move his sleeping place to the little brooder house, give him a house of his own. I swept out the brooder house, which hadn't been used in ten years but which was dry, well ventilated and had four big windows. I built a frame of one-by-eights in one corner and flaked a bale of oat straw into it. Then I called Pat, and he inspected it, indicated that it would be acceptable, and went back to his nap on the lawn. And I knew that a fresh bedroom wasn't going to solve his problems.

I came back to the house, said I was going up on the mountain, slung the field glasses around my neck, and went outdoors again. I called to Pat. He looked up. I said, "I'm going for walk. Want to come along?" He was on his feet in one leap, a changed dog.

I headed for the back gates and Pat took the short cut through the fence and out into the pasture. He looked back to see that I was coming, barked when I opened the gate, and headed for the mountainside. But he stopped half a dozen times and looked back, to be sure I was still coming. Then we reached the far fence and the brush beyond, and he got down to business, more eager, more excited, than I had ever seen him. In that walk across the pasture he seemed to have dropped five years. He was a young dog as he began working the brush patches. Half an hour before that he had been an old dog full of care and worry, the burdens of the whole dog world on his shoulders.

Within five minutes he yelped his signal. He had put up a rabbit. He was off, baying the fresh trail. It was almost two weeks since I had heard his voice, and even running rabbits with Mike it never had the ring it had now.

I went over to where he had started the rabbit and I sat down on a rock and waited. Unless the rabbit ran in, took shelter in a hole or among the safe crannies of an old stone wall, Pat would bring it back to me as he kept it running in its habitual circle.

It was a mild May morning, mild and sunny. The birches were in catkin and small leaf and the maples were in flower, the swamp maples deep crimson across the river, the sugar maples in front of the house a warm amber yellow. Beside the rock where I sat was a clump of pale purple dog violets, and nearby was a single plant of the round-leafed yellow violet. Half a dozen blooms were out, blossoms of warm, golden yellow veined with rich purple.

The rabbit had led Pat over the first rise into the hollow beyond and his voice was muted. I listened, trying to guess where he was, and then I heard a high-pitched hum close by. Changing my focus, both aural and visual, I saw four tiny bees at the purple dog violet clump beside me. They were so small and so busy gathering pollen that I could only guess that they belonged to the *Halictus* family, among the earliest and busiest patrons at the violets' lunch counter.

I watched the bees, there within a foot of my knee, and I thought of the beds of Tertiary fossils at Florissant, Colorado. Among those fossils, fifty or sixty million years old, were bees not essentially different from those buzzing here beside me. In a sense, those bees I was watching had flown directly out of the fossil beds, ancients indeed. And here was I, a relative newcomer on this earth, one of a species probably no more than a million years old, sitting on a rock in the sun, watching them. Getting a glimpse into the remote reaches of time.

I watched the bees, and the warmth of the midmorning sun crept into my bones, and it was good to be alive and up there on the mountainside. I looked down across the pasture and saw the glint of the river through its fringe of elms and basswood just opening leaf bud with that soft green that comes so slowly and vanishes almost overnight. The river danced and sparkled, live water forever on the move. In another two weeks the river would be out of sight from up here, flowing through a green canyon treetop deep. May is a month of swift change.

In the pasture I could see birds searching the grass. Emerald-green grass almost ready for grazing. The birds looked like meadow larks, seemed to strut the way a meadow lark does. I hadn't seen a meadow lark here in Weatogue Valley, though once or twice I had heard songs that roused echoes from my boyhood in the meadow lark country of Colorado. Not quite the same song that I remembered from boyhood, for the meadow larks sing different phrases, east and west; but near enough to be tantalizing. I lifted the field glasses and watched those moving specks in the pasture grass. Sure enough, there was the pudgy body, brown-speckled, the short tail, the long beak, the yellow throat and breast with the dark band across it. And the larks did strut, just as I remembered. Robins strut, and grackles strut, and meadow larks strut, but each in their own manner, unmistakable.

I was still watching the meadow larks when Pat's voice brought me back to the hillside. The rabbit had made its turn and was coming back down the slope to close its circle. Pat was not more than two hundred yards away, telling me with eager voice that he was coming my way.

I turned and watched, and a few moments later the cottontail, already in dark summer pelage, came out of the brush less than fifty yards away. He loped across the clearing, not really hurrying, just keeping safely ahead of the dog. He came directly toward me. I sat stock-still and the rabbit passed me not ten feet away. He turned his head and glanced at me, as though thinking that there wasn't a stump there half an hour before, certainly not a stump wearing a tan windbreaker and a red beaked cap. But he didn't pause to look closer. He hopped on across the clearing and into a patch of hazel brush. But I had seen his big brown eyes and the pink veining in his ears with the sunlight behind them.

Then Pat was yelping excitedly almost in my own ears. He was hurrying along the hot trail, nose to the ground and in full voice. I called to him, but if he heard he paid no attention. He loped on past and into the hazel brush, and as he vanished over the rise just beyond his voice faded again in the distance.

I waited, hoping Pat would come back, content with having brought the rabbit full circle once. I should have known better. Pat was going to run that rabbit as long as the rabbit kept going. He was like the legendary coyote in New Mexico who chased a jack rabbit all one blistering day and when last seen was still at it, though both rabbit and coyote were so tired they were walking.

I waited, and Pat's voice was a faint, distant echo, and at last I went on up the mountainside. Overhead a red-tailed hawk was circling on a thermal updraft, wings set, probably watching the chase and hoping for a kill and a share in a free meal. I left the lower clearings and came to the first stand of white pines, which were steadily creeping down the mountainside and taking more of the old hay fields year by year. At the outer edge the seedling pines were no more than knee-high, still competing with the grass for living space. Then they were high as my head, and the grass was giving way. Then ten feet tall and thick as my wrist. And then the grove of parent pines with trunks a foot through and more, with no grass at all but only the thick mat of needles beneath my feet.

I was just emerging from the pines when there was a rush and a roar of wings almost at my feet. Two ruffed grouse went rocketing away. I had only a blurred glimpse of them before they were lost among the trees, but there was no mistaking what they were. That rush of whirring wings can never be forgotten, once known.

Before they were closely hunted with gun and dog, grouse were known as "fool hens" because they were so unwary. Several of them would sit together in a tree and let a man shoot them one at a time, taking no alarm unless the hunter wounded a bird instead of killing it outright. Then the flutter and fuss put the others to flight. But the grouse's "fool hen" days are only a memory of old men now. I have yet to see one before it takes wing, up in my woods, and once it is flushed it is gone before I get more than a quick glance at it. We speak of grouse as partridges or just "birds," and almost every time I spend an hour on the mountain I put one up. But always the rush and roar startles me. And Pat, who isn't a bird dog in any sense, seems to be equally startled. When a "bird" zooms out of a patch of brush Pat is exploring he sits back on his haunches in surprise, then looks at me, wags his tail sheepishly, and almost asks, "Did you know that thing was in there? *I* didn't."

I flushed the grouse and left the pines and went around a sharp gully and on up the slope. I was in the edge of a stand of gray birches that have overgrown an old clearing when I heard Pat down the hill behind me, yelping a strange call. I turned and listened, puzzled. I had never heard him yelp that way. I watched and waited, and he came out of the pines and around the gully, nose to the ground. Then I realized that he was following my trail. I was in plain sight every foot of the way after he left the pines, but he didn't see me. He was following my scent trail and he didn't look up until he was within twenty yards of me. Then he came to me, nosed my hand, accepted my praise, and lay down, panting.

That was the first time I ever heard his "I'm coming, Boss" yelp, but I came to recognize it as far as I could hear his voice. I might go half a mile from where he left me, but when he quit the chase he would go back, pick up my scent, and follow me. And I always knew, from that note in his voice, that he was coming to find me.

I sat down in the grass and waited for him to catch his breath. He lay there, his ribs throbbing and his tongue dripping, looking at me from time to time with a gleam in his eyes, a look that seemed to say that this was a good world and a good life and we were fortunate indeed to have a part in it. But there was something more in his eyes, something intimate and personal and yet universal. The closest I can come to explaining is to say that it was an unspoken statement of companionship, of something shared beyond friendship.

I have heard it said that man-dog relationships are always

57

those of master and slave. I have heard it argued that the dog, as a species, forfeited its own birthright when it submitted to man's taming. And I have been told that man originally tamed the dog to prove his sense of mastery and that he persists in the ownership of dogs to bolster his own ego. The grain of truth in all these arguments is just big enough to be galling to me when I would answer them. Fundamentally, they seem to me to be an indictment of the men who make the statements rather than of dogs. Furthermore, I doubt that any generality applies, since dogs are as various as are human beings.

I have known a good many dogs, and they have been almost as widely assorted in character as the people I know. As a small-town boy, I had a whole series of pups—none of them seemed to grow to maturity, thanks to poison, distemper and accident. But they were even more varied than the town's assortment of small boys. Some were sneak thieves, some were quarrelsome, some were cowards, and two of them were affectionate, well mannered and self-respecting. Then I became a farm boy and grew up with a collie, who was the best of everything anyone could expect of a dog.

Grown and living on the edge of the country, I had four dogs, one after the other. The first was a wire-haired terrier. He was the only complete coward of his breed I ever knew. And he was the only dog I ever had who sickened and died from distemper shots. Life was just too much for him. Then I had a cross-bred terrier, wirehair and fox terrier, a rough-coated little trouble-maker who took a vicious dislike to the mailman and finally had to be taken to the dog pound and given away. After him came Redge, an Irish terrier and as beguiling a character as ever wore a collar. Redge was grown when I got him, and I should have been suspicious of his immediate acceptance of me. Any grown dog who vows loyalty at the first introduction probably is as fickle as they come.

Redge made himself at home immediately. He was mannerly, friendly, liked children and neighbors, always was ready for a romp or a walk. He was an almost perfect dog for three weeks. Then he vanished. He was gone ten days and he came home with a terrible hangover, starved, disheveled, lame—and apologetic. He was so apologetic that I gladly fed, groomed and salved him.

But in less than a month he was gone again, that time for almost two weeks. And again he came home, hungry, scarred and full of apologies.

This happened four times in six months. I wondered if there wasn't some organization called Vagabonds Anonymous in which I could enroll Redge. Then I had to make a business trip, by car. I wanted company and Redge was a good car dog and a comfortable companion when he was in his domestic mood. I took him along. The second day out I stopped in a town in western Pennsylvania for lunch, and when I had finished I took Redge on a leash for exercise. It was winter and a group of youngsters were coasting down a side-street hill. I stopped to watch them and Redge jerked the leash from my hand and dashed down the hill among the whooping boys.

I searched for an hour on foot, then for half an hour in the car, but Redge had simply vanished. Nobody in town had seen him. So I went to the police station, left a reward and said I would pay shipping charges if he was returned to me. A month later the reward money was returned to me, unclaimed.

After Redge, Ricky was both a relief and a disappointment. Ricky was a Sealyham about a year old. A friend gave him to me, a city friend who had bought him from an expensive kennel as a gift for his wife. His wife turned out to be acutely allergic to dog hair.

I never cared for miniature dogs, but Ricky had the terrier's sturdy vigor and independence that I admired. And he had the courage of Kipling's mongoose after which, in an ironic whim, his previous owner had named him. The only thing Ricky lacked was experience and a sense of life's perils. He never learned that automobiles were juggernauts. I kept him in a fenced yard, where the neighborhood youngsters came to play with him. Inevitably, despite my warnings, one day the youngsters left the gate open. The driver who hit him probably never saw him, for Ricky wasn't much bigger than the crumpled page of a newspaper.

After Ricky, I gave up trying to have a dog. I decided I had known my dogs. Besides, my life acquired complications and my job demanded more and more traveling. But eventually Barbara and I moved up here and settled down. And Pat arrived.

And here I was, this May day, sitting on the mountainside,

Pat beside me saying in his own way that life was good and life was ours, his and mine, whenever we chose to go out together and savor it. And I thought how stupid were those who said that man had made the dog his degraded slave, how completely they had missed the essential relationship of man and dog.

We were only a little way from the springhouse, so I went over to see that all was well with the water supply, which is piped far down the mountain and across the home pasture to the house. Then we followed Springhouse Brook down its rocky gully, I working my way from wet stone to stone, from moss tuft to tuft, Pat exploring the brush, the woods and the old stone walls nearby.

It was that rich time of mid-May when the seasonal overlap of wildflowers was at its best. The damp gully was lush. Late bloodroot bloomed beside columbine just opening flower. There were a few late hepaticas in the deepest shade, and in sun-speckled spots the wild geraniums showed pink in their urgent bud clusters. Early fern fronds spread fine green lace beside late fiddleheads. And violets throve in the brook's misty moisture all along the way.

On the last ledge before the tumbling brook calms itself out across the pasture there is a massive gray ledge worn smooth by the spill of water, which fans over it in a thin, misty waterfall. At the foot of the fall is a small grove of tall, slim white ash trees, and beneath them is a deep bed of rich leaf-mold soil. The sun beats on this small, rich natural garden until the trees are in full leaf and nurtures a thick carpet of early green, bloodroot and wild ginger and anemone and the inconspicuously flowered toothwort. I had found this place in April and thought it should be an ideal place for showy orchis, *Orchis spectabilis,* one of the most beautiful of the wild orchids in this Berkshire area.

I began looking for orchis leaves, which are like darker, shinier copies of the leaves of the moccasin flower or lady's-slipper, the big, showy, woods-loving cousin of the orchis. At last I found two clumps of them, half hidden among the big, smooth bloodroot leaves and the hairy heart-leaves of the wild ginger. There were about a dozen orchis plants in all, and half of them bore flower stalks lifted above the twin clasping leaves. The buds were tight-furled at the top, but most of the stalks had one or two open flowers at the bottom, like hyacinths first showing color. The blossoms were not much bigger than those of garden peas, but their contrasting milk-white and deep lavender made their dainty loveliness altogether beautiful. They were like miniatures of those small spray orchids that delight Barbara at the florist's.

I felt triumphant, the pleasure one has in guessing where a certain wildflower should be and finding it there. I was momentarily tempted to pick one spray for Barbara, but my conscience said a stern "No!" It would wilt within an hour. None of the wild orchids are picking-flowers, and all of them, from the big lady's-slippers to the inconspicuous, single-leafed green adder's mouth, resent picking. Left alone, they flourish. Robbed of even one or two flowers they sulk for a season or two, then vanish. Instead, I picked a few of the strong-scented, brownish-purple three-lipped cups of wild ginger bloom, together with their leaves. The wild ginger has a fragrance that bites the nostril as ginger itself bites the tongue, and the flower is exotic rather than beautiful.

Then we cut across the home pasture to the house.

That afternoon when Barbara and I went for our daily walk Pat ranged ahead of us as usual. But now he merely looked back from time to time instead of coming to nose my hand. He looked back and wagged his tail and went on, no longer needing the reassurance of the physical touch. And he had a jaunty air, a young, lively look and motion that I had never seen before. He seemed at last to be out from under some deeply worrisome burden.

When we turned back toward home, Pat left off his exploration of the roadside field and ran to catch up with us. But instead of nosing my hand he nudged Barbara's leg. She ignored him and he nudged her again.

Back in March, when she occasionally took morning walks alone, she had asked me how to persuade the dogs to go along and stay with her. I suggested that she take tidbits and reward them if they came when she called them. She tried chocolate bits and soda crackers, both of which Mike gobbled greedily and both of which Pat spurned. Then I bought a box of puppy biscuits. Mike, greedily omnivorous, would eat those biscuits as fast as you handed them out. Now and then Pat would accept one, but he made it quite clear that he was conferring a big favor if he ate it. One day when I ran out of dog food I offered them a meal of those puppy biscuits, but Pat nosed them, looked at me in disgust and walked away. He wouldn't even eat them when I had softened them with warm milk.

This day he nudged Barbara, and practically demanded that she dig into her pocket.

"I don't believe it!" she exclaimed. But she reached in her pocket and found two puppy biscuits. She offered one, and Pat took it, solemnly ate it and asked for the other. He got the second one. Then he strutted down the road ahead of us, a dog who owned the world.

The Mike chapter in Pat's life was closed.

CHAPTER 6

OUR VEGETABLE GARDEN has a fence around it but, like every garden fence I ever knew, this one has a gap in it. A small brook which flows until mid-July, then lies dormant until the fall rains, cuts across one corner of the garden and I have yet to find a way to put a woven-wire fence across the brook that will not trap all the floating trash and become a dam that will divert the whole brook right across the corn patch. So I go along with the fiction that the fence encloses the garden, and I rely on the stupidity of rabbits to insure that only occasionally will one find the gap at the brook. Most of the local rabbits are cooperatively stupid. But some other residents aren't.

Frost can, and sometimes does, blight a garden here as late as June, but we have always gambled on the weather. Barbara plants her peas early, since they tolerate frost, and she puts out a bed of lettuce in early May. And we chance a row of beans, a row or two of corn and a few other things before May 15. Thus, about one year out of three, we have a very early garden.

That first year we were experimenting, and we were lucky. By Decoration Day Barbara's lettuce was ready to thin and transplant. Beans were four inches high. Peas were in tendril. Corn was up. Beets made a fine showing. There was only a deceptive green dew of weeds that could be discouraged with a hoe. The garden was all promise and we were full of smug satisfaction. Life was good. The rabbits hadn't found the fence gap at the brook, and the crows hadn't thought our sweet corn worth the bother, with twenty acres of field corn sprouting just down the valley. And the insects were still to come.

On the morning of Decoration Day Barbara went out to survey her domain and talk to her pretty green rows. I was upstairs in my study. I glanced out the window, saw her open the gate, go inside, and stand aghast. Then she yelled, "Hal!"

I knew, from her voice, that there was a bear or a ravening wolf in the garden. She isn't afraid of snakes or minor mammals, including mice and rats, and though she does respect skunks she thinks they are rather amusing—at a proper distance. She yelled again, and I dashed downstairs, picked up the shotgun and ran outdoors. There wasn't a feral beast in sight.

I hurried to the garden gate. "What's the matter?" I demanded. "Where is it? *What* is it?"

"Look!" she exclaimed. And she pointed to her lettuce rows. One whole row was eaten to the ground, and half the next row.

"Look!" she repeated, and pointed to the row of peas, now a row of light green stubs.

And she pointed to the decimation of beets and green beans.

"Something," she said, "has been in here. Something ate the whole garden!"

I went with her down the ravaged rows, looking for tracks. A deer, maybe? But deer leave unmistakable hoofprints, and there were no deer tracks. Birds wouldn't do a job like that. Cutworms would merely sever the stems at the surface of the ground, leave the withered plants. It must have been a rabbit, I decided. Half a dozen rabbits; one rabbit couldn't eat that much.

I started down the center path toward the fence gap at the brook. And suddenly a brown animal burst out of a clump of grass at the corner of the fence. A woodchuck! It dashed along the fence, looking for an opening. I lifted the shotgun and fired, and the woodchuck went head-over-heels, then tried to get to its feet.

There was a yelp from the side yard, then a flash of black and white. Pat, who had been napping on the front steps, raced through the open garden gate, down the path and at the woodchuck. He had it and was finishing the job before I could reload the gun.

The job done, Pat picked up the woodchuck and started back up the path. I intercepted him, and Barbara came over, and I took the dead chuck away from him. Barbara praised him as though he had killed a lion. I said, "Good dog," and let it go at that. After all, I had shot the beast, and another shot would have finished it off. Pat hadn't done much more than pay the tip.

So I took the woodchuck and buried it out beside the big chicken house, and Pat watched me with particular interest. Then he went back to the garden, sniffed the woodchuck's trail, followed it out through the fence gap at the brook, and across the pasture. Barbara got her hand tools and set about repairing what damage she could, and I came back to my typewriter.

An hour later I heard Pat barking down at the lower end of the home pasture where there are the remnants of an old stone wall. I had never heard him bark quite that way before, insistent and angrily excited. I looked out the window and saw him, a couple hundred yards away, dancing about and making a rush from time to time at something I couldn't see. Then Barbara called, "Pat's got something cornered down there in the pasture!"

So I went down, picked up the gun again, and started toward the old stone wall. Before I had gone fifty yards I saw Pat make another rush, saw a flurry of action, and a minute later saw him turn and look at me. Then he picked up something in his jaws and skirted the wall up to the brush bordering the pasture. He had killed some animal and was taking it on an errand of his own. I walked on over to the scene of the kill and found nothing, but under a big stone in the old wall was a den with fresh earth at its mouth. It looked like a woodchuck den.

Pat had disappeared in the brush. I came back to the house, told Barbara what I had found, and returned to work once more.

When I went downstairs for lunch, there was Pat, asleep on the front steps. He heard me, looked up expectantly, and lay there, his tail wagging. I asked, "Where have you been?" and he looked away, and sighed, and went back to sleep.

We ate lunch, and we read the mail, and I went out to the garage. There beside the driveway I found a dead woodchuck. It was neatly laid out on the grass in the sun. I glanced at Pat, who was watching me from the porch. He looked expectant. But I was suspicious. I went out beside the chicken house. The place I had buried the woodchuck we killed in the garden was undisturbed. I got the spade, carried the woodchuck from beside the driveway, and buried it alongside the other one. Pat watched me, and if there wasn't an amused and even smug look in his eyes there should have been.

When I had put the spade away I told Pat that I thought he was a very commendable dog. I did mention that there must have been an element of luck in his achievement, but I added that I would appreciate any help he could offer in keeping down the varmint population, particularly in and near the garden. And I hoped that his luck would continue. He listened gravely and seemed to agree with me, at least in principle.

When Barbara heard what had happened she not only praised him extensively but offered him a whole handful of puppy biscuits as a reward. Pat accepted one biscuit, then walked away and resumed his nap.

The next afternoon I found another dead woodchuck in the front yard, and Pat blandly accepted my congratulations. Then there was a day with no woodchuck. And I am ashamed to say that I was pleased, not because I thought Pat had cleaned out the woodchucks close at hand, but because the perfection peculiar to genius is difficult for most of us—for me, at least—to live with. The next day, however, there was another of his battered trophies. He had left it in a less conspicuous place, beside the tangle of old-fashioned cabbage roses in the side yard, and I did not find it until late afternoon. But anyone with a normally acute sense of smell cannot overlook a dead woodchuck forever, especially on a warm summer day. I found it, buried it with the others, and made my apologies to Pat. I withdrew my suggestion of luck and gave him full credit. After all, it takes more than luck to catch three woodchucks in four days. Pat had provided evidence of skill that possibly verged on genius, and I admitted it.

But that was only the beginning. In ten days he brought in eight woodchucks, and only one of them was an immature young one. It was incredible, for we did not appear to be overrun by the beasts. I had found only two dens in the pasture, both of them some distance from the house. And I had seen only three woodchucks in the open, all three clear across the pasture, at the edge of the mountain. They appeared there in late afternoon, wary and suspicious, and ate grass and clover in the far edge of the pasture. If I stepped outdoors, or even opened a window on that side of the house, they scurried for cover.

Yet Pat had somehow killed and brought home eight woodchucks.

It wasn't until late June that I had a chance to watch him in action with one of them. I was in my study, working, when I heard him bark that morning. He was not far from the house, fifty yards or so back of the woodshed. I thought I recognized the way he was barking, excited but not frenzied, and definitely not summoning help. He had something cornered.

I went downstairs, took the .22 rifle, and hurried outside. Pat heard me coming and barked even more excitedly. Before I reached him he made a rush and I saw that he was trying to overturn a big woodchuck that was crouched in the grass. Pat caught a fold of its loose skin over the shoulders and jerked it off its feet, but before he could get another hold it was on its feet again and snapping at him with long, sharp incisors.

The action was too fast for me to risk a shot. I didn't want to shoot Pat, and he obviously wasn't asking my help. I don't know how he surprised the chuck so far away from a hole, but he did, somehow, and he had it so completely on the defensive that it didn't dare to turn and run for it. So it was fighting somewhat as I have seen a badger fight, though with lesser weapons. The woodchuck's claws and teeth are shorter and less sharp than those of a badger, and the woodchuck is less muscular than the badger of the West. This chuck had found a small hollow in the pasture grass and was hunkered into it, much as a badger hunches into a shallow hole it scratches out with its hind feet in an emergency. There it crouched, turning to face the dog as he shifted his attack from one side to another, meeting every rush with teeth and claws. Though the woodchuck is a vegetarian and in no sense a predator, it can be a vicious fighter. In mating season, in early spring, the male chucks rip and tear each other and sometimes maim or kill a rival for a mate.

66

Pat feinted from one side, then another, dancing about, rushing in, barking to distract the chuck, trying to find an opening. Twice he closed in and caught the chuck by the skin over the tawny shoulders, and each time the loose skin rolled and Pat succeeded only in tumbling the chuck out of its protective hollow. And before he could follow up, the chuck was hunkered in again and facing him with those desperate claws and teeth.

Feint and back, and feint again. Close and snap, and scramble. Despite the infighting, Pat somehow had escaped both the snapping teeth and the raking claws. But the woodchuck was getting tired.

Then Pat closed again, and that time he got what he wanted, a firm hold on the woodchuck's neck. He shook it, as a terrier shakes a rat, and he set his teeth, reached the fatal spot.

The fight was over.

Pat wallowed the dead chuck a little longer, then let it lie and looked at me. He was tired, panting heavily, but he was unmarked. He wagged his tail, and he nosed the dead chuck again, watching for any sign of life.

I gave him proper praise, and I reached down to pick up the chuck and take it to the burying ground. Pat grabbed it by the scruff of the neck and dragged it to one side. It was his woodchuck, not mine.

I walked away to see what he was going to do with it. He picked it up and carried it toward the side lawn. It was a big chuck, quite a load for Pat, who stands only nineteen inches high at the shoulders, and he had to drag it part of the way. But he took it onto the side lawn, over by the cabbage-rose tangle. He left it there and he went on around the house and lay down in the sun. He didn't even get up when I had put the unused rifle in the house and got the spade and took the woodchuck and buried it. When Pat killed a woodchuck he was going to bring it home and put it where his dead woodchucks belonged. After that I could take over, but not until then.

I have no feud with woodchucks as long as they leave the garden alone. If they could resist the temptation of a vegetable garden I would welcome them as next-door neighbors, for they are quiet, cleanly animals of generally exemplary habits. I have heard, and I believe it, that a woodchuck caught young can be tamed into a companionable and affectionate pet.

But a woodchuck is a glutton, and that makes all the trouble. A moderately hungry chuck will eat a pound and a half of green stuff at a meal, and he wants two or three meals a day. That's quite a food budget for an animal which, full grown, seldom weighs more than ten or twelve pounds. And no matter how lush the clover in the pasture, every woodchuck I have ever known prefers to forage in a garden. It takes a lot of young lettuce—or pea vines, or green beans, or beet tops, or cucumber or squash vines—to make up that pound-and-a-half meal. A couple of normally hungry woodchucks can denude even our rather large vegetable garden in a day.

And, since I am drawing up an indictment, I may as well state the whole of my charge. Besides eating as much as half a dozen rabbits do, the woodchuck seems to take special delight in wallowing through or nipping off three times as much provender as he eats. Maybe his other common name, groundhog, comes in part from his swinish habit of spoiling even more than he eats. I've known a woodchuck to cut down a whole hill of squash or cucumbers, then eat only a handful of the succulent tips. And if he finds access to a sweet-corn patch he will pull down a whole row of stalks to get perhaps half a dozen prime ears.

So the "No Welcome" sign is up around here for woodchucks. And, from that very first summer, Pat has helped enforce it. No, I must amend that. Pat *has* enforced it, and *I* have helped from time to time. Actually, I haven't killed more than two woodchucks a year, and Pat has averaged at least a dozen. One year he killed nineteen that I accounted for, and probably several more. That was the year Pat decided to be provident.

I don't know why he expected hard times that summer. Maybe he heard me talking about inflation and high prices. Anyway, one morning I heard him making his familiar woodchuck-at-bay noises at the lower end of the pasture. A little later I saw him skirting the brush, coming toward home at the far edge of the pasture with something the color of a woodchuck in his mouth. He was furtive, but I paid no special attention, thinking he had made his kill and was bringing it home, as usual, to leave on the lawn for me to find. But when I went down for lunch and looked in all the likely spots, I found no woodchuck.

Pat, lying on the front steps, pretended sleep but kept watching me with one eye. Finally I gave up and asked, "All right, where did you hide it?" He lifted his head, yawned, gave me a "Who, me?" look, then turned away. His nose, I noticed then, was still smudged with dirt almost up to his eyes. He had buried his woodchuck.

The next day he brought a woodchuck in and left it, as usual, beside the driveway. Then he buried another one. And that continued for a week. He brought in three woodchucks, and by all the evidence I could see he buried three.

I had no objection to that. My own burying ground was getting rather crowded. But one evening he didn't eat his supper. He had no appetite. A little later we were sitting on the front porch, watching the barn swallows put on their aerial circus in the slow dusk, when Pat came and joined us. Barbara sniffed, and I sniffed. Pat was surrounded by quite an aura, and it wasn't the kind of aura he would get by lying in the mint bed. I got up and went closer to him, and chased him off the porch. Then I began searching for the carcass. I found it behind the garage.

Pat had brought one of his private stock of woodchucks out of storage, and it was well aged. He had not only eaten his fill. He had rolled on it. Pat, for all his virtues, has the idea that well-aged woodchuck not only tastes good but smells wonderful. He enjoys that odor on his own hair and hide. We don't.

I buried the degenerated woodchuck, what was left of it, and I got a pail of warm water well fortified with a strong detergent. I gave Pat the bath of his life.

Pat doesn't like to get a bath, but he submits. He submits grudgingly, grumbling all the while and giving me looks that would blister paint. But now and then there is no other way out. That was one of those times. I scrubbed him from black nose-tip to white tail-tip, sparing only his eyes. Then I rinsed him with three pailfuls of spring-cold water. Finally I let him go. And I made the mistake of standing and watching him.

He stood there, water streaming from him, eyes fairly spitting fire at me. Then he edged even closer to me and shook himself. He shook with every muscle in his body, and I got almost as thorough a dousing as he had had. Then, having his revenge, he rolled in the grass, got up, shook himself again, and rolled again and again. And finally he sprang to his feet, a clean dog, the black in his coat as black as midnight, the white as white as moonlight. He was socially acceptable once more.

It was a week before he dug up another woodchuck. I caught him that time before he had fouled himself as completely as he did the first time, but he got another bath, just the same. And he resented it just as deeply as before.

To this day, Pat can't understand why we fail to share his ecstasy over the smell of ripe woodchuck. He seems to agree that the smell of skunk is objectionable, and when he occasionally has an unhappy encounter with a skunk he submits with good grace to the consequent bath, not even resenting the tomato-juice shampoo that I have found most effective in neutralizing the odor of skunk. But our finicky attitude about the odor of carrion still baffles him. And a bath is an ordeal.

How and where Pat achieved his skill in hunting woodchucks is a mystery to me. I am sure he didn't develop it overnight when he found that we didn't want them raiding the garden. His war with the woodchucks must lie deeper than that, and further back. Perhaps before he came to us he lived on woodchucks—I have never seen him catch or kill a rabbit; but if that were true, he had meager fare after the woodchucks hibernated.

If I were breeding a special woodchuck dog I should choose such stock as must be Pat's, a combination of foxhound and beagle. He has the beagle's excellent nose and stout frame. His legs are sturdy beagle legs but have more length. He has the big, strong feet of a beagle. He has strong jaws and good teeth, and his neck is thick and muscular. His shoulders are heavy, but he has the big-lunged chest of a good hound, which gives him both a strong voice and endurance for the chase. His smooth-haired coat is deceptively heavy, with a thick, fine undercoat that protects him not only from rough winter weather but also from all but the sharpest of raking claws. For such a compact dog, he is remarkably quick on his feet. And he has the courage and persistence of a hound.

Every spring he explores the pastures and nearby brush patches, apparently mapping in his memory every woodchuck hole on the place. When he goes out, even with me, he seems to have a tactical diagram that he follows, skirting the pasture edges, going from one possible woodchuck haven to another, watching always for a chuck that has ventured too far from a hole. He walks with the silent caution of a fox, watching, listening, now and then nosing the air. I have kicked a cottontail out of the grass within twenty feet of him and he hasn't even seen it. He trails rabbits only by scent, never by sight. But with woodchucks he uses every sense.

One afternoon I was walking down the road and Pat was ranging the pasture nearby. I came to a place where a culvert, or sluice as it is locally called, goes under the road to carry the runoff from a shallow gully down to the river. The gully is no more than an open swale where the grass and clover grow lush. Pat came to the upper end of the gully and stopped, alert. He nosed the air, moved a little way, sniffed the grass, looked around. He came toward the road, almost catlike in his caution. He looked again, then he yelped. It was the woodchuck signal. He yelped again and dashed toward the culvert.

There was a scurry and a rush, and a woodchuck raced through the tall grass, also toward the culvert. Pat didn't dash at the woodchuck. He tried to cut him off. But the woodchuck had just enough headstart to beat Pat to the pasture end of the culvert by three feet. The woodchuck dived in, and Pat dived in right behind.

I ran across the road just in time to see the woodchuck streak out of the culvert and plunge headlong into a hole five feet away. Pat was so close behind that he almost plunged into the hole himself. He checked himself, scrambled on down the riverbank almost to the water, then came back and nosed into the hole once and barked a few threats. Then he came back to me, wagged his tail in apology, and returned to the swale in the pasture. There he nosed the ground and seemed to be making mental notes of just where the woodchuck had been, where he had been feeding and which escape route he had taken. I could imagine him planning how to do it differently the next time, how to manage that slight advantage which would beat that particular woodchuck to the culvert.

Whether that is the way Pat's mind worked or not, I have no way of knowing. All I know is what happened two days later.

It was late afternoon, when woodchucks would be out gathering their evening meal. Pat, who had napped in the side yard most of the afternoon, got up, stretched, looked down the valley. He seemed to deliberate for a few minutes, then trotted down the road. I watched, and when I saw that he was heading toward the swale just above the culvert I came in and got the field glasses.

He took his time, but as he approached the swale he became more and more cautious. He slipped through the pasture fence and worked his way into the edge of the swale, head high, tensely alert. He nosed the air, moved a few steps, then yelped. He moved again, yelped again, then dashed for the culvert. I couldn't see the woodchuck in the high grass, and Pat vanished in the hollow at the mouth of the culvert. A few minutes later he came out of the hollow and headed for home, a woodchuck in his mouth.

As far as I could see, at a distance, his tactics weren't much different from those he used when I was there. But somehow he had managed that slight edge, that one leap of advantage that meant victory. Perhaps it was nothing but luck. But he had re-membered that particular woodchuck, he knew the time of day when it probably would be feeding, and he made a successful ap-proach. I am inclined to say that he knew what he was doing and that he had planned it. He had learned from experience and he had altered his tactics just enough to do what he failed to do the first time.

Woodchucks also must learn from experience, but they haven't the intelligence of a wise dog. They have keen eyesight and acute hearing, and they are surprisingly fast on their feet. But if they learn from experience they have to learn fast, for only the lucky woodchucks live to be five years old.

Some woodchucks do show surprising ingenuity. Some years ago I knew a woodchuck that learned to climb over a five-foot woven-wire fence. He could have burrowed under the fence if he had chosen—several of his brothers and cousins did. But this particular fellow learned to climb over, and he did it with a flourish, hand-over-hand, monkey-fashion. Despite everything I did, he lived on our garden for three years. He even seemed to know when I had a gun, for if I was empty-handed he would let me approach within twenty yards before he left off his gluttony and ambled to the fence and up and over. With a gun, I never did get within range of him.

But that was before we came here to live, before Pat came

along to make life precarious for all woodchucks. If Pat had been there, he would have found some solution. I don't know what he would have done, but he would have put an end to that fence-climber's insolence, one way or another. Pat knows more about woodchucks than woodchucks know about themselves.

CHAPTER 7

P AT is so much a dog of the woods and fields that it never occurred to me that he might want to share the river with us. If he had been a spaniel or any other kind of water-loving dog I might have expected it. But not Pat, not a keen-nosed beagle-foxhound sort of dog that would rather run rabbits than eat.

So when I put the boat in the water that spring I didn't even watch Pat's reaction. All I noticed was that he seemed to have no interest in boats. And when we prepared for the first trip upstream to catch a mess of fish he seemed to be bored by what was going on. He sat on the bank beside the dock while we stowed our gear and he had settled down for a nap in the sun even before I cast off.

He was still there when we came back two hours later. He got up, yawned and stretched. He stood and watched while I started to clean the fish, then walked away, totally uninterested.

That evening Barbara said to him, "Pat, you're going to catch up on your sleep this summer." Then she asked me, "Do you suppose he's afraid of the water?" I said I didn't think so, but that he certainly was a dry-land dog. And we began to plan the time we would have on the river.

The Housatonic where we know it best is a broad, placid river close to a hundred yards wide. Its course here, and for several miles upstream, was shaped by a lowpower dam half a mile downstream, where there used to be an electric power plant. Both ends of the dam were washed out by the flood that accompanied the 1938 hurricane, and the power plant was moved and the dam never was repaired. Since then the river has tumbled down twin rapids at the ends of the old dam and resumed its hill-country ways, spilling over the big falls at Falls Village a few miles below and brawling through a rock-studded course in the Cornwalls. But up here, above the old dam, it still acts like a fettered stream. Its channel is broad and deep and its flow is quiet and leisurely except a few times each year when heavy rains or quick snow-melt pour their impatient floodwaters into it. Then it boils and hurries for a few days, full of eddies and flotsam, before it quiets down again. Only once since we have been here, in the hurricane of 1955, has it come over its banks, and then its floodwaters didn't reach our house.

It is a friendly river which shows its temper only often enough to make us respect its power. And it is a special world for us, as special in its own way as the mountainside. Ours is the only house in miles that stands close beside it, so we can go far up-stream and have the sense of knowing a river in a natural world. The few fields and meadows that come down to the river are hidden by the thick growth of trees along its banks. Herons nest beside the river, and black ducks and mallards raise their broods there. Kingfishers rattle and dive and feed on its fish. Turtles sun themselves on its snags. Wild forget-me-nots twinkle in the riverside grass, and wild phlox grows there, and purple vervain and asters and goldenrod.

In the spring we tie up the boat at the foot of a certain meadow and gather very young milkweed for cooked greens. Now and then we go out in the gauzy mists of early dawn to watch the sunrise and eat our breakfast in the boat while we fish for black bass and yellow perch. We go out at dusk to watch the swallows play their games in the sunset sky and know the wonder of the full moon rising over the water. And when fall comes, with first frost, we take pails and nose the boat along the banks where wild grape vines festoon the overhanging alders and basswood trees. We pick tiny river grapes and make jelly that brings all the tang and taste of summer to the winter dinner table.

It's our river, as we say, and we thought, as Barbara said that evening, that Pat would catch up on his sleep that summer while waiting for us beside the dock. And we had no reason to change our minds the next time we went out in the boat, or the next. He watched us go and settled down to sleep, and when we came back he greeted us with a bored yawn.

But the afternoon came when I went out to the garden with a fork and the worm can and he watched me, and when I had dug the worms and started down to the boat he went along. He watched as we stowed our gear, and when I had cast off I wondered why he hadn't lain down for his nap. Instead, he was standing there, alert; and as soon as I headed the boat upstream he trotted up the riverbank, accompanying us.

I watched him, wondering where he was going. We went half a mile upstream and he was still there on the bank, going along with us. We crossed to the far side of the river and anchored at a hole where the perch had been biting the last time we were out. Pat had disappeared in the brush. I decided that he had gone back home to wait for us. We baited our hooks and began fishing.

The perch were there. Barbara soon brought in a fine fourteen-incher and I netted it. I caught a small rock bass and threw it back. Rock bass are a dime a dozen in the river. We were out for perch or big bluegills. Barbara got another nice perch. Then I had a strike and set the hook. As I began maneuvering it in close enough to use the landing net I knew that I had a big one. I was just reaching for the net when I heard a strange puffing noise nearby. I looked around and was so surprised I let my fish have two feet of slack line. There was Pat, not ten yards away, swimming the river.

I felt my line go slack, my big perch gone. Barbara shouted, "There's Pat!" and she missed a strike on her line.

We sat and watched him, surprised, annoyed and amused. He was swimming easily, and he was making for a gap in the brush where the riverbank shelved down to the water. He glanced at us and swam on in, climbed up on the muddy bank and shook himself. Then he turned and almost grinned at us. He shook himself again and went up the riverbank and rolled in a patch of grass.

We looked at each other and laughed. "Well," Barbara said, "at least he didn't try to climb in the boat. Did you know he could swim that way?"

"No," I said, "but all dogs can swim. He's pretty good at it, though. And he judged the current just right." I reached for the bait can. Pat began exploring the brush, apparently satisfied to be on the same side of the river with us.

We fished for another ten minutes, but the perch had moved away. I hauled up the anchor, started the motor and we went slowly upstream to look for another likely hole. Pat heard the motor and came down to the water to see where we were going. He went along, following a game trail through the brush. I anchored again and Pat went off to explore a meadow that sloped down to the river. A few minutes later I heard him yelp that he had put up a rabbit. He trailed it noisily for a little while; then it either ran in or he tired of the chase. He came back to the riverbank, saw that we were still there, and settled down in the sun and watched us fish.

We fished for another hour or so, moving from one place to another, and he accompanied us. Then we put the rods away and leisured upstream another mile, just looking. Pat went along, exploring as he went. Finally I came back to the home side of the river and we drifted on the slow current, back toward the dock. Pat watched us, then came down the far bank till he found a place to his liking, waded in, swam across, and headed for home.

He was waiting beside the dock when we arrived. He greeted us as I tied up the boat, not the "welcome-home" greeting that we got when we had gone off in the car for half a day, full of pleased yelps and whines and prancing leaps, but a shared-adventure greeting. It was more an "I had fun, didn't you?" sort of reception. Then he rolled in the grass, his ultimate gesture of pleasure. I have never seen another dog show an almost voluptuous delight in life as Pat does by simply rolling in the grass or the snow. He puts down his nose and makes a kind of shallow dive. He rolls on one side, then on the other, then lies for a moment in something like quiet ecstasy. Then, if he is on a grassy slope or in a snowdrift, he paddles with his forefeet, a kind of side stroke, and slides himself along, wallowing with some kind of sensual delight. Finally he leaps to his feet and stands as though tingling with pleasure and vitality.

He rolled, leaped to his feet, and he frisked beside me as I took the string of perch to the bench beside the garage to clean them. But his new-found pleasure in the river did not include an interest in the fish. When he saw what I was doing he turned and went to the house. I fileted the fish, took the refuse to the garden and buried it between the corn rows, and we had fried perch for supper. There were a couple of filets left over, and Pat got them. He ate them without enthusiasm. They were just so much crisply fried food to him, and he had already had his customary supper of canned dog food. One thing I could be sure of: Pat would never catch a fish, or dig a carcass out of the garden, and leave it on the front lawn.

Thus Pat established his own pattern for our river trips. He wasn't interested in the boat, except that it was our conveyance on those excursions. He never made a gesture toward getting in the boat. In fact, he has been in the boat only twice, both times in emergencies, and he was uneasy then. He doesn't even like the dock, which sometimes sways, and he will have none of the float to which I moor the boat. The float is a small platform supported by two oil drums. It rises and falls with the water level, and it is somewhat tricky as to footing; and Pat is unhappy even on the bed of a moving farm truck.

I don't think Pat likes to swim. He swims to get across the river, not for fun. Just a little way up the river is a railroad bridge on which he could cross, a stone-piered trestle of stringers, ties and rails over which a locomotive and a few freight cars run every other day. But as far as I know, Pat has never crossed that bridge. Perhaps the gaps between the open ties present more of a hazard to him than the water itself. But I know that he has swum across the river only two or three times when we weren't along.

After that first trip with us, he never let us go without him. He knew what it meant when I went to the garden with the worm can. He would wait beside the gate till I had dug the worms, then accompany me down to the dock, plainly announcing that he was ready to go. Somehow he even sensed when I was going alone and when Barbara was going along. If she was coming, he went back and waited for her. If she wasn't going, he sat and watched me roll back the canvas boat cover. And it wasn't long before he recognized the word "fishing." If he was in the house and either Barbara or I said, "Let's go fishing," he got to his feet and was as eager to go as when one of us said, "Let's go for a walk."

77

Any intelligent dog acquires a workable vocabulary of words that he understands. Some say it is a vocabulary of inflections rather than of actual words, but I doubt that. One day Barbara called to me from downstairs, "Pat thinks you have neglected him this morning. He is looking abused." And I remembered that I hadn't yet given him his breakfast snack. I went downstairs. Pat was sitting in the living room with his most forlorn stepchild look. Simply as a test, I asked, "Do you want to go outdoors, Pat?" He glanced at me and looked away. He didn't want to go outdoors, and he knew that I knew it. And he wasn't playing games. Then I said, in the same tone of voice, "Do you want your breakfast, Pat?" He came to me, tail wagging, and he yawned with a sound that is nothing but a long, "Unnn-rrr," but which does approximate "hungry" if the listener is properly understanding. He makes that sound only at mealtime, and usually in response to the question, "Are you hungry?" A coincidence, perhaps; but a strange coincidence to me. Anyway, he made it quite clear that he didn't want to go outdoors and that he did want his breakfast. So I got his small budget of corn flakes and milk and gave it to him on the back step. He ate it, asked to be let in again, and went to sleep in my study.

I have no intention of going into a doting account of Pat's vocabulary. All I say is that he appears to understand a good many words, as any well-trained dog does. Most of them are connected with his daily habits and our routine, but I suspect that there is something more involved. For example, one winter day when the river was iced over and fishing was obviously not on our schedule, I said, "Do you want to go fishing, Pat?" He looked at me, puzzled, and made no move. Then I asked, "Do you want to go for a walk?" He was on his feet in an instant. We don't fish in the winter, but we do go for walks. It seems clear to me that Pat does not think the two words, "fishing" and "walk," mean the same thing, an outing; and it seems equally clear that somehow he associates the word "fishing" only with the times when we customarily go out in the boat. When I use the word in the winter he seems to know that it has no immediate significance for him. All dogs are practical rather than imaginative in their mental processes, and Pat is as practical as an alarm clock.

So he discovered the river, on those fishing trips of ours; but he made the river valley his in his own peculiar way. In a sense, he made it an extension of his pastures and mountainside, and he remained what he had always been, a dog of the woods and fields. He explored the riverbanks and the nearby pastureland. He followed every game trail through the brush. He startled frogs and turtles, and was startled by them; and he poked his nose into a black duck's nest one day and roused a commotion that sounded like a fox in a farmyard. I hurried over to see what was going on and arrived just in time to see the mother duck chase Pat all the way up the riverbank, her wings flailing and her squawks almost hysterical, and Pat utterly chagrined. Ducks obviously were a brand new experience to him.

There was the day, too, when we heard him just down the river from where we were fishing, yelping his "I've got him cornered" yelp. Thinking he had a woodchuck at bay, I eased the boat down to where he was. And there, in the low grass beside the water, Pat was dancing around a great blue heron, barking excitedly. The heron, three feet or more tall, stood in awkward indignation, first on one foot, then on the other, and darted its long, sharp beak at him, threatening. It didn't seem really alarmed; it was—well, indignant, angrily indignant. And Pat wisely kept his distance. I brought the boat in toward the shore, and the heron heard the motor. It took one darting look, spread its wings and flapped into the air. And Pat just stood and looked, amazed. This strange, gawky creature he had come upon, this peculiar animal that didn't turn and run but just stood there, defying him with that long neck and sharp, darting beak, could fly! He watched it flap down the river, then nosed the mud where it had stood, probably cataloging the scent. Then he looked at me, still baffled, and walked away. Apparently he had never seen a great blue heron. The little green herons, which are much more common along the river, never stood and faced up to him. They took wing when he appeared.

The bird that most annoyed him—and that he seemed to take delight in annoying—was a male kingbird. This kingbird and his mate nested for several years in a willow that slanted out over the river. Father kingbird was typically truculent. The kingbird is one of the toughest, most persistent fighters on wing. Ironically, the only bird that I've ever known to put a kingbird

79

to flight was a ruby-throated hummingbird, a mere smidgen of a bird but one that darted like a bumblebee and utterly routed a kingbird that, not half an hour before, had driven a red-shouldered hawk to cover.

This particular kingbird, the one that nested in the willow, resented anything, man, beast or other bird, that came within fifty yards of his nest. He spent hours on a nearby telephone pole screaming at blue jays and crows. His single-handed attacks on the crows finally drove those that flew up and down the valley to skirt the mountain, a quarter of a mile away. And when we fished anywhere near his nest he warned us off vocally and if we didn't move he began dive-bombing us. He never actually attacked us, but we, like the crows, began detouring his nest area.

Pat, however, refused to be intimidated. Whenever he was in that area he prowled the underbrush right up to the foot of the nesting tree. He never detoured, and the kingbird never stopped screaming at him and trying to drive him away. One day the bird caught Pat in the open and attacked like a demon. How he missed Pat's eyes is a mystery to me. He drew blood on one of Pat's ears, and Pat yelped and snarled and danced as though he had blundered into a hornet's nest. But he didn't run. He snapped and pawed and barked his threats. And the kingbird retreated to the tree and screamed at him while Pat resumed his exploration of the brush.

All that summer they kept up their feud. Pat insisted on his ground rights. Father kingbird screamed and threatened and made token attacks. But to my mind, Pat was the victor. At least he never admitted the kingbird's right to tell him to stay away from that tree and the nearby brush.

We fished and watched the dawn from the water and made a few moonlit excursions on the river, and Pat always went along, always swam across to be near us as we moved from one side to the other. At first I watched when he swam across, thinking he might get into trouble with an unexpected current or submerged brush or that he would miscalculate and come in where the overhanging brush was so thick he couldn't get ashore. But he seemed to know the currents and he always gauged his crossing so that he landed in an open space. I decided that he didn't need my worry.

Then, in September, we had a week of rain. The runoff upstream swelled the river, raised its level four feet and doubled the speed of its current. Several of the brooks up stream were flooded, and every hollow in the pasture was a pond.

Then the rain ceased. I went down to the riverbank to see about the boat. It was still safely moored to the float, its wet canvas cover taut. But there was no sign of the dock. It was under three feet of water. I hauled in on the mooring lines and pulled the float over to the bank, right over the submerged dock. I got an eight-foot plank which would serve as a gangplank, and I told Barbara I was going out in the boat to see the flood upstream. She said, "Not alone, you aren't. I'm going along." Barbara is an excellent swimmer. I'm one of those dry-landers who can stay afloat but shouldn't be trusted too far from land in troubled waters.

So we put on old dungarees and sneakers and I rolled back the boat cover, helped Barbara aboard and prepared to cast off, first making sure the motor would start and the oars were aboard. Then I saw Pat. He was there on the bank, watching, all prepared to go along. Barbara shouted, "Pat! You'd better stay at home!" He wagged his tail eagerly. I shouted, "You stay here! Understand?" He lowered his tail and looked disappointed. I repeated the order, "Stay! You stay home!" And I cast off.

There was quite a current, but the motor took hold and began to fight back. We edged upstream. I watched the currents, found that the flow seemed less in midstream, and worked my way out. We began to make headway. I looked back. Pat was watching but still standing there beside the dock.

We went up under the railroad bridge and fought our way through the strong current boiling in from the Blackberry, normally a tame brook but now a brown surge of foamy water with a good deal of floating debris, mostly small trash. We got through to the quieter water beyond and made our way on upstream. Then Barbara glanced at the left bank and exclaimed, "That dog!" I looked, and there was Pat, tail high, nose eager, following us up the river.

I shouted at him, but he didn't hear me or ignored me. It seemed silly to turn back, just because he insisted on coming along. If he stayed there on the bank, everything would be all right. So I decided to stay on his side of the river, at least not cross, and give him no excuse even to try to swim.

We went another mile upstream, and Pat was with us all the way, having a grand time. Then I had to edge out toward midstream to avoid a current that swept around a jutting bank. I didn't like the look of that current. But before I knew it another current had caught us and carried us toward the far bank despite all I could do. The five-horse motor couldn't make headway against that new current. We were two-thirds of the way across the river when I shouted to Barbara that I was going to put about and work my way back and head for home. The motor had enough power to cut across that current on a long diagonal.

I had just started to put about when I saw Pat at the water's edge. He watched us. We were within fifty feet of the far bank as I turned, and we were still drifting in. He must have thought we were going to stay there or come down that side. He waded in and began to swim, and the current caught him. He turned to face it, fighting his way, but he couldn't make it. He kept trying, but he was carried out from the shore and swiftly downstream.

By then I had the boat headed downstream and was slowly working back toward the other bank. But the current was carrying us faster than it was carrying Pat. I tried to make a course that would intercept him, but it was no use. We were already below him and losing ground. So I put about again, trying to hold against the current. By then Pat had been carried out to the middle of the river. I saw him turn his head and look at us and try to swim toward us. But he couldn't make it. He gave up, turned back and swam with the current, edging his way on across.

But he was tiring. I could see that. Fresh, he swam with his tail-tip out of the water, waving grotesquely from side to side. Now only his head was in sight, and it was low in the water. He was swimming desperately, but making slow headway. He was only two-thirds of the way across, with an even stronger current ahead.

I swung back across the stream and finally got upstream from him. I eased the motor, hoping to drift down and make a grab for him. But the current caught the boat, swung it broadside and away. I raced the motor, felt the propeller bite, and had headway

82

again. Now Pat was within ten yards of shore. But the shore he was approaching was a solid wall of alder brush and red osier dogwood flooded four or five feet deep. If he tried to land there he would get tangled in the brush, and, tired as he was, be sucked under.

I gave the motor full throttle, headed for shore and shouted to Barbara, "Grab the brush! Hold on and we'll try to ease ourselves down to him!"

The boat slanted toward shore. Pat had reached the brush, was trying desperately to get a foothold somewhere. But there was no footing anywhere and the brush was a tangled thicket; he couldn't climb over it or through it. And he was gasping, coughing, very tired.

The boat scraped the brush twenty feet above him. Barbara grabbed an alder, held on, and the boat swung around, stern downstream. I grabbed at an alder tip, missed, grabbed again. The current jerked at the boat. It spun around, and I held onto the alder stem until Barbara caught hold again. And again the boat swung out and around. I was within five feet of Pat. But Pat had given up trying to land there. He was swimming feebly, but he let the current carry him out again.

I shouted to Barbara, "Let go! I think I can get him now!"

She let go, the current caught the boat, and I leaned far overboard, got one uncertain handful of Pat's scruff. I held on till I had hauled him a little closer, then got a better hold. And finally I got my fingers around his collar and knew I had him. But he was at the back of the boat, the motor was racing, and if I let him get six inches closer the propeller would chop his legs. With my free hand I cut off the motor. The boat bounced off the brush, the current caught it and we went end-for-ending downstream.

I was still holding Pat by the collar, and the collar was choking him. He coughed, and shipped more water. I hauled hard, got him head and shoulders out of the water and he got his forepaws on the gunwale. But he hadn't the strength to help beyond that. Then Barbara was there, and the two of us hauled him up, over the transom and into the boat.

He stood there, coughing, water streaming from him, too tired even to shake himself, so tired he was trembling. The boat was out of control, being eddied one way and another by the current. We just missed one floating log, and I saw more logs coming downstream. And we were almost down to the Blackberry and its boiling brown current. If we hit that surging water broadside it could flip us over. I jerked at the starter rope, finally got the motor going again. I managed to meet the Blackberry's current head-on and slice through its turbulence. We reached the somewhat calmer water beyond.

Then we were approaching the railroad trestle and Pat had caught his breath. He gathered himself and shook, so vigorously that he rocked the boat. Barbara and I were drenched. I glanced at her, saw her wipe her face with her sleeve and meet my look with a wry grin. She reached out and rubbed Pat's head and he licked her hand and feebly wagged his tail.

The current carried us past the float and I put about and edged back and alongside. Barbara grabbed one cleat and I made fast, stern then bow. Pat was still shivering, but I was still tying up when he climbed over the gunwale onto the temperamental float. It tilted, almost dumped him in the water again, and he clawed his way up the makeshift gangplank and onto dry land at last.

We followed him. He lay down in the grass and tried to roll himself dry, but he was too tired. He just lay there for a minute, then got up and started for the house. Barbara got an old towel and I rubbed him as dry as I could. He came in the house and lay down on the rug in front of the Franklin stove and stayed there the rest of the day.

It was two weeks before the river had calmed down enough to suggest fishing. We went out, and Pat went along. But he didn't swim the river. Once he waded in a little way, then hesitated, lapped a few mouthfuls of water, and went back. Another time he waded out and swam a little way, then turned and went back. I hoped he had learned his lesson, but at the same time I felt let down. Pat had never before been afraid of anything; and I suppose any man wants to feel that his own dog has all the courage in the world.

The fishing wasn't good. The flood had scoured the best holes and we had no luck. The season was getting late, too, and we didn't go out fishing again that fall. We didn't get in the boat again till after the first frost. Then we got out the pails and nosed the boat up the shore, picking river grapes for jelly. Pat went along, and I kept watching him. He didn't make one gesture toward swimming, even when we crossed the river to come down the far bank.

We drifted down, from one tangle of vines to another. The crop was generous, and I was so busy I forgot Pat. Half an hour passed. Then Barbara hissed for my attention and pointed with her head. I looked. There was Pat, swimming the river. He was just below us, within twenty yards of the shore. He didn't even look around. He was swimming intently, hurrying. He reached the shelving bank, climbed out and shook himself. He stood there watching us. Then he barked, just once, a triumphant bark. "Look, Boss, I did it!" Then he went on up the bank, shook himself again, and rolled in the grass.

I said, "Good dog," and reached for another bunch of grapes. I felt almost as good as though I had swum the river myself.

CHAPTER 8

A COUPLE OF MILES upstream is what we call the Half River area, a low-lying plot in an old loop of the Housatonic left as a slew some years ago when the river cut across the neck and changed its channel. It is rich, fertile land and Charley farms it most years. When the river behaves itself he gets big crops off it. That year he had corn on the Half River lot, and in August he said it would make two hundred bushels to the acre. Then the high water came, covered the corn four feet deep, and when I drove past there two weeks after the water went down it was still a muddy mess. "Not worth trying to get the picker in," Charley growled. "I'll be short of corn, with only the ten acres here at home and about fifteen acres up on Cooper Hill."

A few days later Charley stopped on his way to the village, so mad he sputtered. "What's the matter now?" I asked.

"Why can't they eat that Half River corn?" he demanded.

"Plenty of corn there, and plenty good enough for them! Why do they have to get into the corn right here at home?"

"Who?" I asked.

"They pulled down at least an acre of corn last night. And this morning I was up on Cooper Hill and they're in that too. Damn coons anyway!"

"Coons?"

"Yes, coons! Must have been a dozen of them, the way it looks!"

Pat had heard us and came to see what was going on. Charley shouted at him, "Pat! You chase coons, Pat?"

Pat was busy marking the tires of Charley's truck.

"Probably not," Charley said. "He's a rabbit dog. But all those woodchucks he killed, he might chase coons. We'll try him out and see."

"When?"

"Tonight! Bring him and come up about eight o'clock." And Charley slammed the truck into gear and went roaring down the road, still muttering to himself.

That evening I put Pat in the car and drove up to Charley's. Charley was waiting, with his shotgun and flashlight. And Poochy. Poochy was a shaggy-haired black dog about Pat's size but fatter. Charley thought he had some cocker blood in him, but I couldn't see it.

I let Pat out of the car. Poochy yapped at him and began to walk stiff-legged. Pat growled and his hackles went up. Charley snapped, "Shup up, Poochy!" and I ordered, "Pat, behave yourself!" The dogs nosed each other with grumbling growls. We started to walk across the yard and I thought we were going to make it without a fight. But suddenly they went at each other. Before I could even make a grab they were down, rolling over and over, yipping, yelping and yowling. Charley tried to grab a dog and I tried to grab a dog and we both missed. Then they were on their feet again, snarling and snapping, and I caught Pat by the tail. Charley caught Poochy and we hauled them apart.

Charley said, "Some day they'll have to have it out. But not tonight. Think they've had enough?"

Pat was still quivering with indignation and growling deep

in his throat. Poochy made a pass at him and Charley slapped Poochy across the muzzle. I took Pat to the car and put a leash on him. Charley slapped Poochy again and said, "Let's go."

We walked up the road to his cornfield. Charley flashed his light down the first two rows. Not a coon there. "Coon!" he said to Poochy, and Poochy forgot all about fighting. "Go get us a coon, Poochy!" And Poochy vanished in the corn. Pat whined, wanting to go along, but I kept him on the leash.

We walked down along the corn. Here and there a few stalks were down, the husks stripped back and half the yellow kernels eaten off the ears. "It's worse on in," Charley said. "They took down at least half an acre of it." He was revising his estimate. He stood and listened for Poochy. But Poochy was silent, out of sight. We went on.

We reached the corner of the field. Charley flashed his light again. No coons. Then Poochy yelped, a hundred yards away in the darkness. Charley listened. "Drat that dog! That's a rabbit," he announced. "Don't let Pat go or they'll be gone all night." He listened again. Poochy yelped another time or two, then was silent. "Maybe not," Charley said. "But it isn't a coon."

There was a late moon, but the stars were bright. I could make out the corn rows, the ground beneath our feet, even the trees beyond the field along the river bank. Pat was whining, fussing at the leash. "Suppose he smells coon?" Charley asked. Then he asked, "Does he chase cats?"

"I've never seen him chase a cat. Why?"

"Any cat-killer," Charley said, "will make a coon dog. That's how I got Poochy. A friend of mine down in Bridgeport phoned me one day that there was a dog in the pound that had killed six cats, and did I want him for a coon dog. I said yes, so he got him out of the pound and I went down and got him. Poochy'd never seen a coon, but first time I put him on a coon track he knew what to do. He got me six coons that fall. But his nose isn't as good as it used to be. Last year he tried to take on a porcupine and got a whole faceful of quills. That must have done something to his nose."

Poochy was yelping again, deep in the corn. This time it was excited yelping, and he kept it up. "He's got one!" Charley exclaimed. "He's put up a coon!" He listened. "Bringing him this way!" He played the light along the ground at the edge of the corn.

We watched and listened to Poochy. A cottontail hopped out of the corn and into the light fifty yards away. Its eyes gleamed red in the light. Back in the corn, Poochy was yelping. The rabbit scurried away in the tall grass and Charley yelled, "Poochy! Come here, you dang fool! It's a rabbit! Come here!"

A few minutes later Poochy came out of the corn and panted up to us. Charley said, "Can't you tell a rabbit smell from a coon any more, Poochy?" Poochy lowered his head in shame. But Charley wasn't scolding. He reached down and rubbed Poochy's ears, and Poochy licked his hand; and Charley said, "All right, let's try again." His voice was gentle. "Come on." And he walked down the end of the cornfield a little way and started back between the rows, Poochy at his heels. In the corn, Charley ordered, "Now go get us a coon!" And Poochy trotted off into the rustling darkness.

We walked the length of the corn rows, and Poochy didn't put up a thing, not even a rabbit. Charley sighed and called Poochy in, and we went back to where we had started, where the coons had taken down the corn the night before. Charley said, "Let's see what Pat can do."

I took the leash off Pat and Charley snapped it on Poochy's collar. We took Pat to the down stalks and Charley said, "Coon, Pat. Coon! Go get us a coon!" Pat sniffed at the half-eaten ears and wagged his tail eagerly. "By golly!" Charley exclaimed, "I think he's got the scent! Go get 'em, boy!"

Pat started down the corn row, sniffing loudly. Poochy whined, wanting to go along. "You just let Pat have his chance," Charley scolded. "You didn't get anything!" And we waited.

Pat vanished in the darkness. We stood there listening. Five minutes. Ten. Then, from off across the field, Pat began to yelp. Charley listened, then turned to me. I said, "Rabbit." I listened as Pat's voice rose in his trail cry. I shook my head. It was the same cry I'd heard a hundred times on the mountainside.

We hurried down through the corn to the far end once more. Pat was still crying trail out in the corn. Then he was coming toward us. Charley switched on the light, played it along the edge of the field. Another minute, and there was the cottontail, caught in the light as it hopped out of the corn and scurried across the grass. Twenty yards behind came Pat, nose to the ground, yelping eagerly.

I shouted at him. "Pat! Come here, Pat!"

Pat paid no attention. He was on a rabbit trail. Charley added his voice to mine, but it was no use. Pat vanished in the darkness. His voice thinned away in the distance.

Charley looked at me and grinned. We went out into the grass and sat down to wait. Charley lit a cigarette and I filled my pipe. And Charley talked about coon hunts in the past. About the time Poochy ran a big old buck coon all over the valley in the moonlight and finally up onto the ridge. Charley was about to give up when Poochy yelped that he had something treed. So Charley climbed the ridge, and up there he found not one coon but three treed in the same tall pine. And he told about the night when Poochy ran a coon into a hole among the rocks on the ridge, and Charley got up there and urged him on and Poochy went right on in. "There was the dangdest row you ever heard. Sounded like seven tomcats fighting in there. Then one coon came tearing out of there, and I shot him. And before I could reload, here come another one, Poochy right after him. That one treed close by, and I got him too. Oh," Charley said, "Poochy's earned his keep, all right. Haven't you, Poochy?" And he rubbed Poochy's black nose.

We sat for twenty minutes, and Pat didn't come back. Twice I heard him, up the valley, and each time his voice died away. At last I heard him behind us, over toward the ridge, yelping a trail again. "Well," I said, "Pat's a good rabbit dog, but—"

"But no coon dog," Charley said. He got to his feet. "Let's go back to the house. He'll come in, when he gets tired."

So we went back to Charley's house, and we sat and talked for an hour, and had coffee, and waited. At last Poochy, who had been asleep there on the floor, lifted his head and barked once. He got to his feet and went to the door. Charley turned on the outside light. There was Pat, muddy to his ears. He barked happily when he saw me. Charley said, "He's been up in the Half River. He couldn't get that much mud anywhere else! Want a rag?"

I wiped the worst of the mud off of him, got the old Navy

blanket from the trunk and put it on the car seat. As I let Pat in I said, "Well, now we know. Pat's not a coon dog."

Charley grinned. "How about we take him out after rabbits next week? Up in back of your place."

I got behind the wheel and we drove home. Pat nosed my hand and seemed to think he deserved praise, not censure, and I agreed, at least in principle. As I took him out to his house I told him it didn't matter about the coons. Poochy, I said, didn't find one either, and Poochy was a real coon dog. I heard Pat's tail thumping, satisfied. Then he settled down in the straw.

Barbara came downstairs to have a before-bed snack with me. "How many coons did you get?" she asked. "Enough for a coat?"

"Pat," I said, "chased rabbits for an hour and a half. And Poochy's nose wasn't working tonight. Not one coon."

She laughed. "I'd rather have sheared beaver anyway."

"If Pat and I have to catch it," I said, "you'll have to settle for lapin."

"Beaver or nothing." Then she said, "I'm glad Pat didn't chase any coons. He's got enough to do around here now, what with woodchucks as well as rabbits."

One morning the next week Charley phoned and said, "Good day for rabbits. How about it?" I told him to come on down. I changed to old khakis, put a handful of shells in the pocket of my canvas hunting coat and took down the shotgun to run a clean rag through the barrels. Pat heard me and came to see what was going on, all eagerness and excitement.

I don't know whether Pat can smell a gun or just senses it when I take a rifle or the shotgun down from the pegs in the old pantry that we use as a catch-all closet for outdoor clothes. But all I have to do is take down a gun and here he comes. Even if he is upstairs in my study, somehow he knows what I am doing. I can no more sneak out of the house with a gun than I can open a can of dog food without his knowing it. He has ears like a fox, or he has some sixth sense.

He came and sniffed the gun and whined and danced with joy. He dashed to the door, then back to me, then to the door again. I put away the wiping stick and went out on the front porch with him, but he couldn't contain himself. I said, "We've got to wait for Charley." But Pat didn't want to wait for anyone. He raced around the house, toward the pasture, then came back to see what was keeping me. I sat down on the steps in the sun. Pat sat down in the grass. But he couldn't sit still. He went out to the road, around the house again, back to me, sat down, got up, rolled in the grass.

When Charley arrived Pat greeted him with a flurry of barking. Charley got out with his gun and Pat sniffed it and raced for the pasture, circled, came back, and raced off again. "Full of beans," Charley said. "He sure wants to go, don't he?"

We started across the pasture, Pat racing ahead of us, then coming back, then hurrying off once more. He could hardly wait. But once he was assured that we were really going, he settled down and began working. There wasn't much chance of putting up a rabbit in the pasture, but he wasn't missing any bets. He worked every grass clump as we went. Then we were at the brush on the far side, and anything could happen. Just beyond the pasture fence is a tangle of wild blackberry, hazel, viburnum, goldenrod, chokecherry and seedling pasture cedars, perfect cover for rabbits. But there wasn't any rabbit there that day.

We crossed the fence and started up the mountain, past the first few big pines and the tall sumac tangle just beyond. We were just emerging from the sumac when Pat sounded off. I have never heard him quite so loud and triumphant. He had put up a cottontail. I saw the rabbit, just for an instant, a hundred yards on up the slope. Then it was gone in the brush. And Pat was racing after it, yelping magnificently.

It was a good day, bright sun that had not yet swept the dew off the grass. Mild as only a New England autumn day can be, the sky clear as glass. You could see twenty miles. I thought I could make out the individual trees on Canaan Mountain eight miles away, though it must have been clumps of trees that I saw.

The dampness made good trailing. The scent clung. And Pat's nose was fresh and eager. He went belling up the mountainside, and the slopes threw back his voice in a wonderful assortment of echoes. Charley turned and grinned at me and shook his head, delighted. Then he stood and listened again to the music Pat was making.

We listened, knew that the rabbit was making a big circle, and

91

we sat down on a rock in the sun to wait. Charley said that now Pat was up in the birches where they cut sawlogs ten years ago— "Those no-good gray birches, or whatever you call them." Now he was in the hollow where there used to be a big fox den—"I trapped four big reds out of that den one winter." Now he was on that low rise with the twin seep springs on the near side. "Used to be woodcock in there every year, but I haven't seen a woodcock in a long time . . . Uh-Oh! He's turned! Rabbit's made his turn and is coming toward us now. You ready? I'll back you up. We've got to get him for old Pat!"

Pat's voice was clear and true now, coming down the long slope. I was on my feet, gun ready. I moved to a spot where I could see the whole breadth of the clearing.

Closer and closer came Pat's voice. He was only a hundred yards away now. Out of the corner of my eye I saw a movement off to my left. I swung around just as the rabbit hopped into the open. He hesitated, looked around. Charley was right behind me. "See him?" he whispered. "There he is!"

I had my gun at my shoulder. The rabbit started across the clearing. I swung the gun just past him, squeezed the trigger. The rabbit went end-over-end.

Pat emerged from the brush just as I shot. At the roar he yelped twice as loud. Charley shouted triumphantly, "You got him!" And then Pat was at the rabbit. He nosed it and turned to me, panting, almost grinning. I said, "Good dog. Good dog!" And he came over and nosed my hand and went back to the rabbit.

Charley said, "Well, that's number one." He picked up the rabbit, said, "Fat," and handed it to me. I put it in the game pocket in my coat, and we went back to the rock and sat down to let Pat catch his breath. We discussed the fox-rabbit cycles, the way foxes increase steadily for a few years and pretty well thin out the rabbits, and then the foxes get rabies and other diseases and die off and the rabbits come back. The main cycle is about every ten years, with lesser cycles of around three and a half years. Charley said that seemed to tally out. A few years back there were foxes all over the place. They got so numerous he saw two out in his calf pasture beside the house in broad daylight one day and shot them both. "Scrawny things, mangy, looked half starved." And the next year there just didn't seem to be any foxes at all. And the rabbits began to come back. Now the rabbits were building up.

"The foxes are coming back too, aren't they?" I asked.

"Yes. But not as fast as the rabbits."

"Foxes don't breed like rabbits. And they only have four or five kits in a litter, usually."

"That's right. And I suppose the foxes will come back and clean out the rabbits, and we'll start all over again."

Pat was on his feet, ready to go. We started on up the hillside. Charley said, "There used to be quite a few snowshoe rabbits up on the ridge here, but they got thinned out too. Suppose they'll come back?"

"They should."

"Wish Pat would put one of them up today. A snowshoe would give him a real run. But they're away on up, if they're here at all."

We climbed to the next shoulder of the mountain, and there, in a patch of shoulder-high briars, Pat put up another rabbit. He went yelping off across the next hollow and Charley and I climbed to a bare ledge where we could look down on the whole briary tangle. That rabbit made a small circle. Pat brought it back within ten minutes and Charley got it with one clean shot.

We hadn't gone another hundred yards when Pat was off again in full tongue. We moved over to take a stand, and I heard Pat yelping in frustration. No trail cry, that. "He's got something cornered," I said, and Charley said, "Maybe."

We hurried off to see, and we found Pat at an old stone wall, trying to tear the wall apart. He wasn't getting very far, for it was one of those old walls built of big stones, some of which must have weighed a good half ton. The rabbit had a hide-out there, and not even a bear could have reached it. I found a stick and poked in, but it was no use. We gave up, and finally we persuaded Pat to give up.

As we went on up the mountainside I said I couldn't figure how even a bull-shouldered farmer could move such stones and build a wall like that. "They levered them onto a stone sled," Charley said. "Or if they couldn't do that they hooked a chain around and dragged them out with two or three yoke of oxen."

"That must have been a long time back," I said. "There haven't been any oxen used around here in your lifetime, have there?"

"Sure have," Charley said. "Just over the ridge, on the slope of Cooper Hill, the Nowell brothers worked cattle up into the 1920s."

Pat had put up another rabbit, and while we waited at the stand Charley told me about the Nowell brothers, Later I pieced out the story from others who remembered the Nowells, crotchety, hermit-like brothers who worked a small farm on the Massachusetts-Connecticut line only three or four miles from my place.

The Nowells, John and Matthew, hadn't much use for modern ways. They lived in a well-worn house and kept apart from the world. They farmed with oxen and lived on what they grew or hunted. Now and then one of them would hitch up a span of oxen and take a few bags of oats to Canaan and trade for salt and coffee, but that was their only contact with the twentieth century.

Then Matthew died and John lived on there alone, more than ever the hermit. Until, one winter night, all of Cooper Hill and probably Tom's Mountain echoed with the bellowing of the Nowell oxen. They made such an uproar that neighbors went the next day to see what was wrong. They found John Nowell dead in his house, several days dead, and the oxen were starving for water. There was a little flock of chickens, wild as partridges. And there was a clowder of cats, twenty or more of them, spitting, clawing and threatening everyone in sight. But finally the neighbors got things in hand, took John Nowell's body out of there and gave it a decent burial. Whether he liked it or not, John Nowell had his last ride in a motor-driven hearse. And that was the end of farming with oxen around here, though the Jacobs brothers, Hyman and Pepoon—I think that's a wonderful name, Pepoon—kept oxen on their small farm in the edge of Canaan a few years after that and occasionally yoked them to a plow. But that, apparently, was mostly to entertain outlanders, who were coming up here for vacations even then.

Pat brought another rabbit around, and I got it. Charley said, "I wish we had time to go on up and see if he could find one of those snowshoes, but it's getting toward noon. Anyway,

it'll be better for snowshoes when there's snow on the ground."
So we started back.

Pat found another rabbit and brought it around for us on the way down the mountain, and Charley got it. Pat was getting tired, but he made it quite clear that he thought it had been a wonderful morning. And we had done exactly what he expected us to do. We had got four rabbits in front of him. Pat was proud of us.

We went home, and Charley said, "We get a light snow, we'll have to go out again. After snowshoes. See if they're still up there." He stopped to rub Pat's ears, almost as proud as though he owned him. "Don't know that I've ever run rabbits with a better dog." Then, as he was getting in his car, "Ever want someone to take him off your hands, just let me know."

Two weeks later I got word from an editor asking if I would go down to Florida on a writing assignment. Barbara and I talked it over. It was a job I wanted to do, and we could drive down and make a pleasant trip of it. There was only one real problem; Pat. I said, "We could put him in a boarding kennel." And Barbara said, "Pat's not a kennel dog, and you know it. It would break his heart." I agreed, and I put off the decision. Then I remembered what Charley had said.

The next day I drove up to see Charley. I told him we were going to have to make a trip and I wondered if he would keep an eye on the house. He said sure he would and he asked when we were going. I said not till after Thanksgiving.

"How long you going to be gone?"

"A month, maybe six weeks."

Charley looked disappointed. "Then we won't get a chance at those snowshoe rabbits." He thought a moment, then asked, "What you going to do with Pat? Take him along?"

"I thought of putting him in a kennel."

"Kennel?" Charley snorted. "Pat in a kennel?" He laughed. "He'd get out the first night, if he had to tear the kennel apart. Why don't you bring him up here?"

"You mean that, Charley?"

"I told you if you ever wanted anyone to take him off your hands just to let me know, didn't I?"

"Not for keeps, Charley."

"All right. But you let me have him while you're gone."

"I'll pay his board."

Charley laughed at me and walked away.

CHAPTER 9

EVEN BEFORE we began packing for the trip south, Pat became uneasy. I don't know how he senses these things, but when we talked about details in the evening he lay there staring moodily at the fire and listened to us instead of stretching out and napping. He cut short his morning excursions and spent more time at home. He followed me upstairs and down. When I went to the village on some errand he watched me off, apprehensive. When Barbara and I both went he showed every sign of being worried, and when we returned he greeted us with special fervor.

Then I brought down the suitcases from the attic and Barbara began putting clothes into them, and Pat sulked. I packed the car, and he stood and watched with a downcast look that was close to accusation. That evening he didn't want to go out to his house to bed. I urged, then ordered, and he went, but with every sign of hurt and disappointment.

The next morning when I put the leash on him he said very plainly that he knew he was being abandoned and that though he might forgive me, in time, he would never forget. He got in the car with a sigh of resignation and a look as sad as a homeless bloodhound. I took him up to Charley's.

Charley greeted him with delight. "Well, Pat! Going to live here for a while, are you? Come on, boy." And he rubbed Pat's ears. Pat didn't respond at all. "We're going to get us some of those big white rabbits," Charley promised. Still no response.

Poochy appeared, saw Pat and bristled. Poochy yapped. Pat glanced at Poochy, then dismissed him. He was watching me, his eyes accusing. Poochy came over to him, growling. Pat didn't even get to his feet. His hackles rose a little, but he didn't make a sound.

I got back in the car. "Don't worry about Pat," Charley said. "Have a good trip."

I came back home, got Barbara and the last of the luggage, and we took off. She asked how Pat had liked it up at Charley's. "He accused me of abandoning him," I said. "Did everything but call me a louse."

"I almost wish we'd brought him along."

"A dog's a nuisance on a trip." Then I added, "I wont be bullied by a dog. Or tied down by one!"

Barbara glanced at me and smiled. I said, "Forget Pat. This is a fun trip as well as a work trip. Nobody asked him to move in on us. After all!"

We drove all day through the wintry countryside. Several times Barbara mentioned Pat, and I said, "Forget him. He's all right." Once, in a little town in Delaware, I saw a black and white dog that looked so much like Pat that I turned and stared, and missed a road marker. I had to go back and find the route. And Barbara laughed at me and said, mocking me, "Forget him. He's all right."

That evening we stopped at a motel in Maryland. After we had eaten and returned to our room I said, "I'm going to call Charley."

"About Pat?"

"About the back door. I'm not sure I locked it."

"I'm sure you did. I saw you."

"I think I went out that door later, for something."

"Well, go ahead and call. Make sure."

I put in the call. Charley's wife, Elitha, answered. As soon as she knew who was calling she laughed. "Calling about Pat, I'll bet. Well, Pat's all right. He's here in the kitchen right now. Wait a minute. Here's Charley."

Charley came on the phone. "Hello. So you're worrying about Pat. Well, stop worrying. He and Poochy had a set-to, like I said they would some day. Poochy jumped him and Pat gave him a roughing up. Lots of noise but no blood. I guess they got things settled. I'm taking him out after those white rabbits tomorrow. How's the weather down there?"

When I had hung up, Barbara said, "Everything's all right?"

97

"Fine," I said. I told her everything Charley and Elitha had said.

"And the back door—"

"Oh, I forgot all about that. Well, I must have locked it, as you said. Charley will go down in a day or two, and he'll find out if I didn't."

Then it was nine o'clock, Pat's bedtime, and I started for the door before I remembered. I picked up a road map from the dresser and went back to my chair, and we planned the next day's drive.

It wasn't until we reached St. Augustine that I stopped thinking, involuntarily, that nine o'clock was Pat's bedtime. Then the beach, and the sun, and the job I had gone down to do took over. We went inland to Orlando and visited friends, and I gathered more material. Over to Daytona and on down the coast, and finally back to the Orlando area again, to a cypress cottage on Lake Sheen near the village of Winter Garden. We settled down to do the job we were there to do.

Christmas passed, a strange Christmas and very different from the one the year before. The only Christmas tree we had was a conventionalized little pine I outlined on a window with green Scotch tape. We decorated it with tiny balls taped to the fake branches. The Christmas cards from up North only made us homesick. The card from Charley and Elitha said, "Plenty of snow and cold. Better stay there till spring!" Then a P.S.: "Pat's fine." We read it and laughed, then were silent. Finally I said, "I wonder if he'll know us when we get back." And that evening we remembered last Christmas, there in the valley, the snowstorm, the howling dog; and Barbara said, "My Christmas present —the dogs!"

We went back to work at the typewriter the next day. Before the week was out the job was finished. We were tired, so we decided to stay on for another month, for a vacation. After all, it was, as Charley and Elitha had said, cold and snowy up home. Down here we had a cabin on a lake, good bass fishing, and a boat. It was one of Florida's chilly winters, but we had a fireplace and a small gas heater. We fished. I fed the fireplace. And the chill rains came. We wearied of fishing. We watched the weather reports from up North and kept telling ourselves how lucky we were.

Then, one morning when the fireplace was utterly inadequate and the fog from the lake hung thick and dank, I said, "I'm going in and have the car greased and the oil changed."

"Why?" Barbara asked.

"Well, it's almost time to change the oil, and—"

"I'm ready to go any time you are," she said.

"You want to go home, too?"

"Of course! I didn't want to mention it if you wanted to stay, but—"

"I didn't either, if *you* wanted to stay. . . . Start packing. I'll help when I get back with the car."

We headed north the next morning.

We struck the first snow in Maryland, just enough to whiten the ground. By the time we reached New Jersey it was four inches deep. We crossed the George Washington Bridge and headed north, and there was six inches of it, with dirty drifts flung up at the roadsides by the snowplows. Then we were in the hills, coming up Route 22, and Barbara exclaimed, "Isn't it beautiful!"

We came to the broad valleys where the hills stand apart, and we made the turn at Millerton, crossed into Connecticut, passed Lake Wononscopomuc at Lakeville, a glittering expanse of virgin snow ten inches deep that lay like a gigantic frosted mirror among the wooded hills. On to Salisbury village.

We stopped in the village to buy milk and eggs and butter and bread, and chops for supper. And Barbara said, "Dog food. Don't forget that." It was our first reference to Pat since we had left Florida, and even then we didn't speak his name. We hadn't had word from Charley or Elitha in three weeks, not since Christmas, and the thought was in both our minds that even if nothing had happened to Pat he might not want to live with us any more.

I bought half a dozen cans of dog food, and we put the groceries in the car and came on up over Smith Hill, where the whole of the Taconic range can be seen. The mountains gleamed in the late afternoon sun, majestic and enduring as time itself. Ahead lay the long ridge of Canaan Mountain. Then we saw Tom's Mountain, with its peculiar knob at the top, the gray shadow of its naked trees dancing with the glitter of snow

99

beneath. Then left, up Twin Lakes road to Weatogue, and up our own valley. Past Albert's farm, with the snow a foot deep in his fields and the barn faintly steaming with the warmth of his dairy herd. Past our own lower pasture and along the iced-in river sealed in snow and looking like a white, winding, multi-lane highway. And there stood our own red buildings, our big gray barn, our towering Norway spruce like an enormous green candle flame beside the house. Home.

I got out the key to the front door, carried in the groceries, turned up the thermostat and listened for the furnace to go on. Barbara was bringing in an armload of the miscellaneous duffle that accumulates in the back seat on any long trip. The house was cold, down in the fifties. I said, "Let's let it warm up." She said, "Let's." Still we didn't mention him by name.

We got in the car again and drove up to Charley's. We pulled into the yard and two dogs came running from down by the barn. Poochy and Pat. They dashed up into the yard and stood barking at the car. Pat, who used to recognize the sound of our car half a mile away, who used to come running down the road to greet us. Now he just stood there and barked, as at total strangers.

We got out of the car. I called to Pat, but he wouldn't let me touch him. He approached with his hackles half up, suspicious. Barbara spoke to him. He hesitated, wagged his tail tentatively, then came and sniffed at her outstretched hand. He came and smelled me, and looked at me, and suddenly stood on his hind legs, his forepaws on my arm, and nuzzled his head against me. He whined softly.

Charley came up from the barn, where he had been preparing for the evening milking. He shouted a greeting, shook hands. And Elitha was at the door, calling, "Come on in where it's warm! Welcome home!"

We all went inside and sat down. Pat came and nosed my hand, then went to Barbara, then lay down and watched us. Elitha got coffee and we sat and talked for a little while, and Charley said he shot ten rabbits ahead of Pat before Christmas. Hadn't been out but once since then. Too much snow. No, they hadn't found any of those big white rabbits, the snowshoes. Didn't know what happened to them.

And finally we got up to go. "You may have to tie him up

for a few days," Charley said, "to keep him at home. But I'll let you know if he comes back up here." He leaned down and rubbed Pat's ears fondly. He looked up at me. "If I didn't have Poochy, I think I could persuade Pat to stay here. But one dog's enough." He grinned. "At least, we'll keep him here in the valley." Then he looked at Pat and shook his head. "Dangdest notional dog I ever saw! You know what he did? The week after Christmas he went down to Albert's. I went down and got him, and he went right back. Decided he was going to stay with Albert. By Gosh, he stayed there almost a week! Didn't come near this place. So I said, 'All right, if you like the meals better down there, stay, drat you!' But he was just visiting. After four, five days he came back here, and he's been here ever since. But almost every morning he takes off and goes down there. To see old Teddy, or maybe the new pup Albert's got. Gone for a couple hours, then comes back. He knows the whole valley, by now, thinks it's *all* his, I guess."

We went out to the car. Pat went with us. He got in between us on the front seat and sat there, serious as could be as we started home. Then he nosed Barbara's arm and turned and shoved his nose under my arm and snuggled there, whining softly. And sat up, self-conscious, and stared at the road.

I put the car in the garage and we got out. Pat dashed to the front porch, barked at us happily, came piling down the steps and raced to us and around us, and back to the porch. I opened the door and he surged in, swept down the hallway, around through the living room, down the hallway again, his claws rattling on the bare floor. Then he went to the rug in front of the Franklin stove and lay down, claiming his place. Pat, too, had come home.

That evening the temperature dropped sharply. It had been only ten above zero when we arrived, and by eight o'clock it was down to five below and still falling. Nine o'clock, Pat's bedtime, and Barbara said, "I think he had better sleep in the house tonight. It's too cold out there in his own house."

I agreed. He had been sleeping in the barn, up at Charley's, with the heat of forty cows warming it up. So I spread an old blanket for him in the living room and told him that he was a very privileged character. But he didn't seem to understand. We came upstairs and unpacked the big suitcase, and he followed us up, settled down in my study. I said, "All right, if that's what you'd rather do, sleep there."

We got ready for bed. Pat came to the bedroom door and whined. "What do you want, anyway?" I asked. He went to the head of the stairs and waited. "All right," I said, "go on downstairs and sleep." But he didn't go.

"Maybe he wants to go out," Barbara said.

"He's been out." But I took him downstairs, opened the front door for him. He turned away. He didn't want to go outdoors. I took him to the blanket in the living room and ordered him to lie down. He lay down, reluctant, and I came back upstairs.

We went to bed. Half an hour later Pat wakened us, whining. I put on a robe and slippers and went downstairs. He greeted me happily and went to the back door. "Want to go out?" I asked. No response. He looked at me as though I were being very stupid. And then I asked, "Do you want to go to bed?" He wagged his tail and made it quite clear that was what he wanted. He didn't want to sleep in the house. He wanted to go out to his own house, his own bed, cold or not.

I went back upstairs, pulled on my pants, put on my boots, threw a coat over my robe, and took him out to his own house. The snow was up to my knees and so cold that it whined under my feet. I opened the door, flashed the light inside, saw that there was plenty of straw. Pat went in, nosed into his familiar nest in the straw and lay down, content. I closed and latched the door and went back to the house, looking at the thermometer at the back steps. It showed nine degrees below zero.

It was eighteen below when I got up the next morning, one of those brittle winter dawns when the sky looks like ice and the whole world seems ready to crack if you gave it one sharp blow. The ice on the river was booming from time to time. The sun came up accompanied by brilliant sun dogs, patches of frosty rainbow set on each side of it close to the horizon.

I dressed and set the coffee to cook. Then I pulled on my boots, buttoned my heaviest coat and went out to Pat's house. He heard the crunch and whine of my footsteps and began to bark, the eager greeting bark. I opened the door and he dashed out, raced in a circle on the heavily crusted snow, flung himself headlong and rolled and slithered down the little slope toward the driveway, then leaped to his feet and raced me back to the house. His breath made steamy little clouds in the frigid air. We came inside and he went to the foot of the stairs and lay down in front of the hot-air register to soak up the heat.

Half an hour later I gave him his breakfast snack. And forgot all about tying him up. He ate and went out to the road, and I remembered. I went to the door to call him, but he had already started down the road, toward Albert's. His tail was high, his head alert. He owned not only this valley but the whole world. I didn't have the heart to call him back and tether him. Anyway, he wasn't going up to Charley's. I let him go.

Two hours later he was back, at the front door asking to be let in. He came up to my study and lay down, just as he had been in the habit of doing before we went away. I wondered if he was telling us, in the only way he could, that if everything was the same with us, he was glad to have things unchanged with him. He was willing to take up where we left off if we were. And that afternoon when we had to go to the village for grocery staples he stood on the front porch and watched us go with no sign of doubt that we would soon come back.

On the way, we stopped at Albert's to say hello to Albert and Ruth, his wife. They asked about the trip and we discussed the weather. And I saw their new pup, Suzy. She was gangling, all legs and tail, but puppy-cute and affectionate. I asked if she was a German shepherd, and Albert said, "No! Her mother was a black and white hound, looked a little like Pat. I don't know where Suzy got that color." And he said he'd had her spayed.

Ruth said, "Speaking of Pat, he was the cutest thing. That week he came down here to live, we thought he'd decided to stay here till you got back. Charley came down and took him home, but he came right back here. So we fed him and he played with old Teddy and Suzy. Then after about a week he moved back to Charley's. But he came down every morning to visit. He was here this morning for an hour or two."

"He gets along all right with Teddy?" I asked.

"Oh, you know Teddy," Albert said. "He makes a lot of noise, and sometimes they wallow around, but they get along."

"If Pat makes a nuisance of himself," I said, "let me know."

"We will," Albert promised.

And Ruth said, "I don't mind him at all. He comes, and if Suzy isn't out, Pat comes to the door and whines for her. I let her out and they go romping in the snow till Pat decides he's visited long enough. Then he goes back home."

"I hope," Albert said, "that Pat teaches Suzy to catch woodchucks, come spring. How many did he get last year?"

I told him, and he said, "More than I got with the gun." He laughed. "Send him down here next summer, will you? The woodchucks in that patch of alfalfa across the road will keep him busy all summer long."

Pat settled down without a lapse and without any hesitation that I could see. It surprised me, since he had been a wanderer before he came to us. I would have been disappointed, but would have accepted it, if he had chosen to go back to Charley's after we got home. I would have understood if he had gone down to Albert's to live. But apparently he had made his choice, and despite our desertion of him for those long weeks he had accepted the situation and was going to continue to live right here. At least when we were here.

I can only guess at what goes on in a dog's mind, and I doubt if anyone can do much more. But if I can judge by Pat I would say that a dog's sense of home is primarily linked with the person or the people who live there. Cats, I believe, have less of a sense of personal loyalty, though cat-lovers may, and are quite welcome to, dispute me on this point. But once a dog has established his loyalty to a person, he will go anywhere with that person, and it is that person's presence which seems to stand for "home." The place factor seems to me secondary, though as long as it is associated with the person it remains the dog's property, too. Pat, for instance, obviously considers this house not only ours but his as long as we come back to it regularly. If we are gone for a week or more and he is staying somewhere else, his ownership somehow is canceled for that time.

Albert stows hay, straw and other things in our big barn. Charley uses our corncrib to store his excess. Both Charley and Albert are here every day or so on some errand, and when we are here Pat announces them with his usual announcement barking, then goes to greet them. He knows and likes them both. If we are away overnight, however, and either of them comes here and even approaches the house, Pat acts as though they were total strangers. He warns them off, bristles, even threatens them. How Pat knows the difference between an overnight trip and an absence of a week or more, I don't know, unless he knows that when we take him to either Charley or Albert and drive away we won't be back for a while.

Whatever goes on in his active mind, he knew that we had come back to stay, and that this was home again, for all three of us. He went up to visit Charley every now and then, but never stayed more than an hour or so. He went down to Albert's almost every morning. But he came home for meals and he stayed at home nights. In his own house. He didn't mind the cold out there. He certainly preferred it to what we considered the comfort here in this furnace-heated house when it came to be bedtime. Nine o'clock in the evening and if we were alone he got up from his rug, stretched and came to me and indicated that it was his bedtime. If we had guests in for the evening he would wait till nine-thirty before he made his move. Sometimes he would even wait till ten. But if they were not gone by then he would get up, stretch, yawn ostentatiously, and come over to me. If I tried to ignore him he went back and sat down and looked bored. Sometimes he stared at the guests as though asking, "Don't you know enough to go home?" It became a joke with our close friends. When he got restless or sat there staring at them, someone would say, "Pat is telling us it's time to go home." With this lack of tact, he has cut short a few pleasantly leisurely evenings. He has also put an end to a painfully dull evening, now and then.

So Pat established this new pattern for himself. This was home again, but every day he went visiting, down the road or up. And as the winter wore away he made most of the valley his own. One day I took the back road up past Bartholomew's Cobble to Ashley Falls, in Massachusetts, and up there in the woods, three miles from home, I saw him trotting along the road ahead of me. He was obviously just out for a look at the country, taking his time and stopping to investigate the whole roadside. I slowed the car and loafed along a quarter of a mile behind him for a way. Then he heard the motor and turned and looked. As I drove closer he began to wag his tail. He moved off to the roadside and waited till I came up. Then he greeted me politely, as much as said he didn't want a lift, and I drove on. When I looked back he was coming up the road again, still exploring. I didn't see him when I came back that way, but he was at home before noon, his jaunt completed.

Everyone in the valley knew him by then. I asked various ones if he was making a nuisance of himself. They said no. "Once in a while he stops past, and if we are outside he says a polite hello. But he never stays more than a few minutes." Then they laughed. "He's a very busy dog. He seems to think he has to patrol the whole valley."

But only on our side of the river. There is a highway bridge about three miles below us, but nobody beyond the bridge ever reported seeing him. And though he usually traveled by road, he was careful about cars. Only twice have I known him to be in danger on the road, and both times it was my own fault. Once we were walking along the road and a big truckload of gravel approached, hurrying. I didn't think Pat saw the approaching truck, for his back was to it, and I called to him. He turned to look at me, and I shouted, "Pat, come here!" He heard the alarm in my voice and started across the road, right in the truck's path. The driver hit the brakes, tires squealed, and Pat, thanks to quick reflexes, leaped almost from under the crushing wheels. The other time we were walking just at a bend in the road and Pat was sniffing some scent in the road. Again his back was to the car that came whooping around the curve, and I shouted at him. He looked at me instead of the car, and once more he was saved only by his quick reflexes. The car brushed him as he leaped away, just nudged him. After that I stopped trying to warn him. I only confused him when I shouted that way. And never since then, to my knowledge, has he had a close call.

He explored the valley, and January passed and February brought a touch of warmth. The snow thinned to a crust, the ice went out of the river, and before the first of March the sap had begun to flow in the maples. I knew the sap was beginning to move even before I saw the first sap buckets out because the red squirrels were busy in the big sugar maples in front of our house. And after the squirrels came the chickadees. The squirrels, following some calendar of their own, knew when to nip the latent buds on the maples and open tiny taps on the branches. They ate the buds, as spring salad I suppose, and then they sat and licked the sap as it oozed out, drop by sweet drop. And the chickadees, perhaps by watching the squirrels, knew what was happening. They followed the squirrels and got their own spring sweetening from the little oozing wounds on the maple branches.

March blew and blustered toward the equinox. April was at hand, and the first crocuses showed color and the early bees were out. One sunny day I took the boat out of the garage and cleaned it out and sanded the bottom and gave it a first coat of paint. Charley came down with a spreader full of manure for the garden, but said it was still too wet to plow. The swamp maples were in crimson flower and there was a thin haze of delicate green on the white birches on the mountain and the elms beside the river.

I noticed that Pat had curtailed his trips up and down the valley. Now he was limiting his trips to the morning visit down to Albert's, to see Suzy. He had more urgent business here at home, though I didn't realize it until the day, the first week in April, when I saw him lying on the front steps, looking smug and triumphant. Sure enough, when I went out to the garage, there was a dead woodchuck on the lawn. Spring was here. The woodchucks were out and foraging, and Pat was back at work.

CHAPTER 10

SPRING in New England is seldom much to boast about. Robert Frost summed it up when, speaking of an April day, he said that if the sun is out "you're one month on in the middle of May," but if a cloud comes along "you're two months back in the middle of March." Fall is our season up here, often extending from Labor Day clear through to Christmas. We sometimes say that we earn that superlative fall by enduring the punishment of spring. One raw April day I asked Fred, at the hardware store in the village, if we weren't going to have any spring. "Oh, it'll be here," Fred said. "It's a little late this year. Usually it falls on a Monday, but this year it won't be till a Tuesday. Leap year."

So, the year I am speaking of, we endured April. Pat brought in the first woodchuck, and the next day it snowed. Charley spread the load of manure on the garden, and it was two weeks before he could get in with the plow. I tried to fork up a row for Barbara to plant peas, and I found frost still in the ground four inches down. She planted them anyway, and somehow they sprouted. I painted the boat and slid it over a scum of ice at the river's edge to launch it.

Then it was May, and the next thing we knew the temperature was in the eighties and the pear tree was showing white and the apple trees were all pink and green. The ducks were quacking on the river, Barbara saw four bluebirds and we had our first mess of milkweed greens. Albert began planting field corn.

Pat's visits down the road, at Albert's place, lengthened from an hour or so to most of the morning. Then I heard him running the lower slope of the mountain, not back of the house but down the valley, back of the lower pasture. I asked Albert if he knew what was going on. He said he wasn't sure, but Pat was coming down there every morning, getting Suzy, and going off somewhere. Yes, he had heard Pat on the mountainside. And yes, it was fawn season. He didn't know whether Pat was running deer or not, or if Suzy was running with him.

I went down there to watch. Sure enough, Pat and Suzy were running the mountainside together. But only the lower slopes, and apparently they were running rabbits. Suzy, slim and young, ran like a deer, but she ran without a sound. It looked to me as though she were just running with Pat, and Pat was doing all the trailing. But it still bothered me. I remembered what Dave, the dog warden, had said, that one dog alone seldom will run deer but that two of them together might.

I mentioned it to Charley. Charley said, "No. Pat doesn't run deer. Last winter, up after rabbits, I jumped a deer and I tried to put Pat on the track, just to see. He wasn't interested at all, wouldn't even trail it. No, he's chasing rabbits. Lots of them around, this year."

I wasn't convinced. Then, one morning, Pat himself answered the question. He went down to see Suzy, and half an hour later I heard him in the lower pasture. He was barking his "something cornered" signal. And another dog was barking too, a dog with a shrill, high-pitched voice. I took the .22 rifle and hurried down to see what was going on.

I came in sight of Pat just in time to see the end of the fight. Pat and Suzy had a woodchuck cornered. Suzy was dancing and barking and diverting the chuck's attention. Pat closed in and finished the job. Then he picked up the dead chuck and headed for the fence row. Suzy bounced beside him, yapping triumphantly.

I turned and came back home.

The next day they caught another woodchuck down there. Before the week was out Albert reported that they were busy in that patch of his alfalfa that had been overrun by chucks the year before.

I came home and told Barbara. "Let's see," she said. "Suzy's a pup. Mike was a pup. Do you suppose Pat just *has* to have another dog to look after and train? Or does he just need a playmate and hunting companion?"

"I don't know," I said. "But if Suzy wasn't spayed—"

"But she *is* spayed. I doubt that sex is the answer. Anyway, Pat must be old enough to be Suzy's grandfather."

"Some day," I said, "I must explain some of the facts of life. Dog life. Fritz, the collie I had when I was a boy, fathered a litter of pups when he was fourteen years old. The mother was a setter less than two years old. . . . But, as you say, Suzy is spayed."

Pat and Suzy worked on the woodchucks in the alfalfa field for three weeks. I don't know how many they cleaned out of there, and Albert said he lost count. Suzy, who apparently never learned to trail rabbits, despite Pat's lessons, learned about woodchucks. She was light-footed as a fox and fast as a whippet. One morning on my way to the village I saw the two of them there in the alfalfa, and stopped to watch. They were working the field about twenty yards apart. Suddenly Pat stopped, sniffed, stiffened. Suzy came to attention, watching him. Pat barked twice. A woodchuck scrambled toward a den. Suzy streaked toward it from one side and Pat from the other, cutting off escape. The chuck was cornered. Both dogs closed in, barking, and the woodchuck couldn't watch them both at the same time. Suzy found the first opening, closed in and made the kill.

I drove on, thinking that every move Suzy made was a move I had seen Pat make. Pat was a good teacher, and Suzy was an apt pupil.

By mid-June they had cleaned out the alfalfa patch and Pat had turned his attention to the home pasture again. Some mornings he brought Suzy up to hunt with him, and some mornings he hunted alone. His particular quarry was a big old grandfather chuck who lived in the fence row across the pasture back of the house and who sometimes came out to sun himself on a low ledge of rock that we had named the Resting Rock because we often sat there when we walked in the pastures. He was a cagey old boy and seemed to offer a special challenge to Pat. I sometimes thought that he taunted Pat by sitting there on the rock till the very last minute, watching Pat make his stealthy approach, then darting to his den just one jump ahead of Pat. It could have been a game, though I doubt that even canny old woodchucks ever play such games.

Pat was out there one morning, looking for Gramp, as we called the big chuck, when a strange yellow dog appeared from the brush up on the mountain. Pat barked a few times, then went closer. They nosed each other, and I saw Pat begin to strut. The other dog acted coy, dancing away, then waiting for Pat to approach again. I thought, Uh-oh! and I went outside and called to Pat. He was reluctant to come. I went part way across the pasture, ordering him, and finally he came toward me. The other dog followed. Just as I had suspected, she was a bitch. A nondescript little yellow bitch with so many strains mingled in her that I couldn't even guess at her ancestry. And dirty and scrubby looking. But a bitch.

I took Pat by the collar and led him home. The yellow bitch followed. I put Pat in the house and closed the doors, and I went out and told the strange dog to be on her way. She backed off and whined, and I picked up a stick and tossed it at her. She turned and ran. Things had been thrown at her before. I chased her out to the road, tossed gravel at her, and she trotted up the road, looking back from time to time. I stood and watched till she was out of sight. Then I came in, telling myself that was that.

Pat wanted out. I told him to go lie down. He whined, begging, and I chased him up to my study and closed the door. He whined a little while longer, then quieted down. I told Barbara what had happened and warned her not to let Pat outdoors. We kept him in all morning. I took him out on a leash after lunch, then brought him inside again. And somehow forgot to hook the screen door.

Pat lay down, accusing me of cruel and unusual punishment. I said, "You stay home today. Understand?" He glared at me.

I came back to work. Half an hour later I heard the screen door slam. I went downstairs. No Pat. I looked out. No Pat. I went out to the road, and there he was, trotting up the road, tail high and every step intensely masculine.

Well, I thought, let him go and get it over with. He'll be back for supper. But, I thought, I do wish you had better taste in women, Pat. That little yellow bitch!

Suppertime came, and no Pat. Dusk, and no Pat. Dark, and he still hadn't come home. Barbara asked, "Hadn't you better go look for him?"

"No. He'll be back in the morning. He'll have his spree and come crawling home, full of apology."

"I wonder," she said.

She was right. Morning came, and no Pat.

I waited till ten o'clock, then got in the car and cruised up the road. He was nowhere in sight. I stopped at Charley's. Charley was at the cow barn. I greeted him and he said, "Looking for Pat?"

"Yes."

Charley jerked his head toward the river. "He's down there, in a patch of brush. With that yellow cur-dog. Been there all night."

"Raising a rumpus?"

"Quite a rumpus," Charley said. "I was going to call you."

"Who does she belong to?" I asked.

"Never saw her before."

"I'll go down and get him."

Charley laughed wryly. "I tried to, myself. At two o'clock this morning. Couldn't get near him. Chased them out of there and came back to bed, and in half an hour they were at it again, yowling and yipping. I almost got out the shotgun."

"Why didn't you?"

"Well—" He sighed. "Go see if you can get him to come."

I went. I hadn't any trouble finding them. They were in a patch of alders not far from the riverbank. Pat heard me coming and broke away and backed into the brush. I called to him, then ordered him. The yellow bitch scuttled away. Pat turned and followed her. I followed the two of them, ordering Pat to come. He didn't come, but finally he stood and waited while I went up to him. I snapped the leash on his collar and started back to the car. He came along without a struggle, until the yellow bitch began to whine. Then Pat lunged at the leash, did his best to get free. I held on and finally he gave up. But he whimpered his complaints and his entreaties all the way back to the car. The yellow bitch followed halfway, then turned and went back to the alders.

Charley said, "So you got him. Better tie him up for a few days, I guess. . . . What's got into you, Pat?"

Pat glowered at him. When I had spread the old blanket on the seat and urged Pat to get in, he struggled at the leash again, tried to bolt. I wore him down, got him in the car, closed the windows and drove home. Out of the car, he whined and begged, finally stood on his hind legs, put his forepaws on me and pleaded. It was no use. I got a rope, tied it to his collar and tethered him in the yard. He sat down, disconsolate, and I came in the house.

Five minutes later he began to howl, the most mournful howl you ever heard. I went out to him, and he begged again to be let loose. I said, "Not a chance. Settle down and get over it." And I came back inside. Pat began whining and slowly built up to the howls again. Barbara, at her typewriter, said, "Now I know where Mike learned it! Isn't there anything we can do to stop him?"

I went outside and scolded and threatened him with a whipping. He cowered and lay down and looked away, as much as saying, "Go ahead. Beat me. Either let me go or beat me to death!" And I said, "Melodrama won't get you anything. Shut up and stop this nonsense!" I came back indoors.

More whining. Then silence. I thought I had finally won. Then I looked out. Pat was gone.

I went outdoors again. He had chewed the rope in two. Pat, who could be tethered with a string!

I picked up the leash, got in the car and drove up the road. I caught up with him, just below Charley's place. He heard me coming, though, and left the road, looking back only once. Then he scuttled across the field toward the alder brush beside the river.

I parked in Charley's barnyard again. Charley saw me and asked, "What happened?" I said, "He chewed the rope," and I went down to the riverbank, angry and determined.

It took me half an hour to catch him that time, and when I had him on the leash he tried to grab the leash in his teeth and bite it in two. I slapped him across the muzzle, finally discouraged that idea, and hauled him back to the car and took him home. That time I got out the chain we had used on Mike. I chained him up.

He whined and howled and struggled with the chain all that afternoon. Life wasn't worth living around here. I wore out a weekday edition of *The New York Times* trying to slap some sense into him, and still he howled and struggled at the chain.

Suppertime and I put his food out for him. He wouldn't eat. Barbara suggested that maybe a walk would help. I said I doubted it, but I was willing to try anything. I took the leather leash, snapped it on his collar and started out, walking down the road. He balked. He didn't want to go that way. We had a bit of a set-to, and he finally sulked along behind me for fifty yards or so. Then he jerked back, almost pulled free. I grabbed the leash with both hands, and he took a step toward me, got a bit of slack, caught the leash between his teeth and cut it cleanly in two. Then he spun and dashed up the road.

I got out the car and went after him again. That time he and the yellow bitch ran up the river as soon as they saw me coming. I chased them half a mile before I even made Pat slow up and listen. It was almost dark before I got the lead chain on him—I had taken the chain that time, not trusting either hemp or leather.

Charley was waiting for me at the car. "I just called the dog warden," he said. "He'll come and get her first thing in the morning. That should put a stop to it." He looked at Pat. "Lord, I never saw such a notional dog! Pat, you are the dangdest determined dog I ever knew!"

I had to wrestle him into the car, but I got him home safely. I took him to his house, put him inside and closed and latched the door. I dragged myself to the house, tired out. "For a dime," I said to Barbara, "I'd tell the dog warden to take Pat, too."

"It's been a rough day," she said. "You'll feel better after a good night's sleep. I suppose Pat has his rights, too. Wasn't it Dryden who said, 'Love endures no tie'? Well, Pat certainly proved that today!"

"Pat," I pointed out, "doesn't know Dryden from Deuteronomy. And as for love, did you see that scrofulous little yellow bitch?"

"Only from a distance. But I've seen men make utter fools of themselves over very peculiar-looking little, uh, girls. Haven't you?"

I was in no mood for argument or persiflage. I took a shower and she made me a sandwich and poured a glass of milk. I began to feel somewhat better, could almost believe Barbara when she said Pat probably would be all over it by morning.

We came up to the bedroom. I opened the window, and I heard Pat whining. Just as they had that morning, the whines built up to howls, long, drawn-out howls that had the melancholy of all time in them. I shouted to him to be quiet.

He was quiet just long enough for me to get stretched out in bed. Then the whining began again, slowly building up to heart-rending cries. I started to get up. Barbara said, "Let him cry. He'll get tired after while. I can take it if you can."

Ten minutes and the howls subsided. I began to drift off to sleep. Then the whining began again. I tensed, waiting for the whines to become howls. They did. And eventually they subsided again.

That went on for an hour. The crying would cease and I would think at last he was going to quiet down for the night. I would yawn and settle down and begin to drowse, and if Pat didn't actually begin to whine within five minutes I roused knowing he would. He did. Over, and over, and over.

Finally Barbara asked, "Are you awake?"

"Of course I'm awake!"

"I just thought, maybe he's hungry. He didn't eat his supper."

"You think he's howling for *food?*"

"He could be, couldn't he?"

"No!"

"Sometimes when I can't sleep I get warm milk and crackers."

I didn't answer.

"I'll warm some milk if you want to take it out to him."

I still didn't answer.

"Are you asleep?"

"No! Pat doesn't want warm milk!"

"Then I'll take it out to him." She got out of bed.

I sighed, got up, shuffled into slippers, put on a robe. And took the warm milk out to Pat's house. I opened the door a crack, and had to brace myself—Pat lunged at it, almost knocked me down. Finally, blocking the entrance with my own body, I shoved the pan of milk inside and slammed and latched the door. There was a bang and a clatter and I knew the milk was all over the floor. Pat was no more interested in milk than I was in—well, in the Einstein theory, at that moment. I heard him kicking the empty pan around, and I went back to the house. He was crying before I got inside.

That was a night. Along about three o'clock in the morning I thought he was going to tear his house apart. I was sure I heard splintering timbers and the bang of a battering-ram. And then, for some reason, silence. I drowsily thought he had either broken his way out or killed himself, and I didn't care which. I went to sleep.

I slept till almost seven o'clock. When I got up I remembered the night and went to the window and looked out. Pat's house was still there, seemingly intact.

I dressed and went downstairs. I set the coffee to cook. Then I went outdoors, out to Pat's house, to see if he was still alive.

Pat wasn't there. The door was open, the latch broken. He had flung himself at it until it simply gave way. But that was minor damage. The inside was a wreck. I hadn't been wrong when I thought I heard timbers splintering. He had torn up the boards that framed his bed, literally splintered them. With his teeth. He had torn strips off the two-by-fours that framed the house. He had frantically ripped at the door frame. This awed me. But the frenzy in him was shown by a minor thing. I had stowed half a roll of roofing paper in a corner of the house. He had attacked that roll, torn every foot of it to bits. The whole floor was littered with straw and torn scraps of roofing paper. A tornado couldn't have done much more to the place. The only thing he had missed was the windows. Why he didn't leap at the glass panes and break his way out simply, was a deep mystery.

I came back to the house, told Barbara what I had found, had a cup of coffee, and got in the car and drove up to Charley's.

"Get some sleep?" I asked him.

"Till about three-thirty. What happened?"

I told him. He shook his head, unbelieving. Then he said, "But I guess it's all over now. Dave was here just a little while ago. He got that yellow bitch and took her away."

"Pat?" I asked.

"He's down in the brush, was a little while ago. He wouldn't come to me, and Dave didn't try to catch him."

I went down to the brush and called Pat. He crawled out of a patch of weeds, looked at me accusingly, and came to me with the worst hangover I think I ever saw. I put the leash on him and started back to the car. He could hardly walk, he was so weak, and he was the utmost picture of dejection and defeat.

I put him in the car and brought him home. I fed him, and he ate a little, lay down for ten minutes, then ate again. I chained him in the side yard. He slept all morning, exhausted. I fed him again, then cleaned up his house, built a new box for his bed, burned the wreckage, the old straw and the torn-up roofing paper. I put new straw in, and I repaired the latch. Then I took him out there and put him to bed and locked the door.

He was quiet all afternoon. That evening I let him out and fed him again. I came in the house just for a minute, and when I went outside he was gone, his meal half eaten. I waited half an hour and he didn't come back. Then I went up to Charley's again. Yes, Charley said, he saw Pat cut across the lower pasture, down to the alder brush, about half an hour ago. And even while we stood there talking, Pat began to howl, down there in the brush.

I went down and got him.

He cried off and on all that night. The next morning he was tractable enough, though he looked at me as though I had beaten him with a club. I fed him, keeping him on the chain, and then I gave him a bath, for he was disreputably dirty. Then I brought him in the house. He lay on his rug, licking himself and refusing to look at either Barbara or me. We were the enemy, the cruel, cruel jailors. He hadn't a kind look for either of us.

I let him out at noon, and he started up the road. I followed him in the car, caught up with him just below Charley's place, and ordered him in the car. He got in, glaring but submissive. Back home again, he lay and glowered at us. When I let him out for supper he ate, then started up the road again. And again I brought him home. That night he howled only half a dozen times.

For two days that continued. Once he got all the way back to that patch of alder brush, and he was so surly when I went after him that I wondered if he would bite me. He didn't, but he made it quite clear that we were no longer friends. Not even acquaintances, for that matter, He was a prisoner, and nothing more.

After three days of it I said to Barbara, "It begins to look hopeless. I don't know what to do."

"He just doesn't like it here any more," she said. "What do you do when a dog gets that way?"

"Get rid of him. We've tried everything." We had. We had petted, pampered, humored, pleaded, and got no response from him. None. Life wasn't worth living, certainly not here with us. If I let him out and off the leash, off he went. Back to that patch of brush, where he skulked and howled.

I went to the phone, called Dave, the dog warden. I told him what had happened. "What do you want to do?" Dave asked. I told him I didn't know. "Has he turned vicious?" No, I said, though I wasn't sure that he mightn't if this went on much longer. And Dave said, "I'll come up and we'll see."

Dave arrived, in his pickup truck with a stout cage in the back. His little girl, about six years old, was with him. Dave told her to stay in the car. I brought Pat out, on the chain, and Dave looked at him and said, "He's a nice dog. I wouldn't put him away for anything." He held out his hand and Pat sniffed it and looked away. The little girl shouted, "Daddy, can't I get out and play with the doggy?"

Dave glanced at Pat, considered for a moment and said, "All right, come on."

She got out of the car, ran to Pat. Dave watched, alert. So

did I. She rubbed Pat's ears, then hugged him, and he turned and licked her face once. She laughed, and Pat looked away. I drew a deep sigh of relief. Dave said, "Take the chain off of him." I loosened the chain. Pat looked around, at all of us, and went out to the road and trotted away, up toward Charley's.

I glanced at Dave and he nodded, and I shouted at Pat. He glanced back and hesitated, then went on.

We caught up with him half a mile up the road and brought him back. Barbara had come out. "What are you going to do?" she asked. "You're not going to—to destroy him, are you?"

Dave shook his head. "He's too nice a dog to destroy." He thought for a minute, then said, "There's a farmer over in New York that wants a dog. A nice man. How about if I take him over there?"

I looked at Barbara. She looked at me, then at Pat. "Pat," she whispered. He didn't even look up.

"How far away is this farmer?" I asked.

"Forty, fifty miles." Dave looked at Pat. "He's a farm dog. He ought to like it there. Nothing wrong with him, really. He just doesn't like it here, I guess. Not any more. He blames you for what happened, apparently. And he might turn vicious with you."

I nodded. That's the way it looked to me. And there was no use prolonging it. "All right," I said, "go ahead. Take him away."

Dave helped his little girl into the truck. He came back and reached for the lead chain, led Pat to the car, opened the door and urged him in. Pat climbed in, got up on the seat beside the little girl and sat down. Dave tossed the chain to me, glanced at Pat and his little girl, smiled, and started the motor.

"Send me a bill," I said.

Dave grinned and shook his head.

Barbara called, "Pat! Good-bye, Pat!" Pat didn't even look around. Barbara turned and hurried to the house.

Then they were gone.

I put the chain away in the woodshed, and I went in the back door. Barbara was at the kitchen sink, just standing there with the water running. She had been crying. But she turned to me with a smile and asked, "What do you want for lunch?"

"Anything," I said.

She turned off the water. "She was a cute little girl. Darling! What was her name?"

"I don't know. Dave just called her Honey."

"Why don't we just have a salad? I'm not hungry."

"I'm not either."

And suddenly she burst out, "He wouldn't even look at me when I said good-bye to him!"

"He had other things on his mind."

"Salad and a sandwich. How about deviled ham?"

"That'll be fine."

She turned to me. "Well, say something! Talk about him! Say you're sorry! Say something!"

"What is there to say? Of course I'm sorry. He was a gentleman, and we knew him for a while, and now he's gone away. It's all over with."

She opened the refrigerator, stood there, forgetting what she wanted to get. She slowly closed the door. Then she said, "It's a lousy shame! There should have been something we could do about it!"

"There wasn't."

She opened the refrigerator door again, got out a head of lettuce. "You'd better phone and tell Charley."

I called Charley. He said, "I guess that was the only thing to do. We'll miss him." Charley didn't want to talk about it either.

I came back to the kitchen. Barbara was making the sandwiches. "At least," she said, "he didn't put him in that cage. That would have been awful, to see him go in that cage."

CHAPTER 11

R EMOVE one member of the household and the absence is felt everywhere you turn. When I got up the next morning and had set the coffee to cook I automatically went outdoors and started to Pat's house, only to remember and turn back. When I had eaten breakfast I reached under the dish closet for the box of corn flakes to prepare Pat's morning snack, then set it down again. In my study, at the typewriter, I would write a page or two, then look up, wonder where Pat was, listen for him downstairs, asking to be let in. And in the evening, when nine o'clock came, I instinctively looked for him to come and say it was his bedtime.

Barbara missed him as much as I did. The second morning we were in the garden, she thinning carrots, I hoeing German weed out of the sweet corn. She sat back on her heels, pushed the hair out of her eyes with her wrist, and said, "How do you suppose he learned not to step on the plants in the garden?" It was uncanny, the way he could run full tilt across the garden and not step on one plant.

"For that matter," I said, "how did he learn the word 'garden'?" If he started to cross a flower bed, all I had to say was, "Garden, Pat," and he turned aside.

Barbara sighed and went back to her thinning.

That afternoon we went out in the boat. We were anchored upstream, lines out, fishing for perch. Some movement caught my eye. I looked up, saw a kingfisher dive with a little splash. And Barbara jerked around, looked, then caught her breath and shook her head. "I thought I heard him swimming the river," she said. And when we came home at dusk we both were watching for him, expecting him to be waiting at the dock.

Charley stopped past. We talked crops and weather, both of us avoiding the subject we wanted to talk about, both refusing to mention it. He drove on.

Albert was less reticent. I didn't know why, at first. He hailed me as I was on my way to the village. "Sorry to hear about Pat," he said. "Hear you had to send him away."

I said yes. To a farm over in New York State.

"Suzy stands and waits every morning and can't seem to understand why he doesn't come. She's lonesome, I guess, with old Teddy gone too."

"Teddy? What happened to Teddy?"

"I had to put him away. Poor old fellow got sick the other night and I called the vet. He said it wasn't any use doctoring him, old as he was. He was fourteen. That would be eighty-five or ninety in a man, wouldn't it?"

"Around ninety, I think."

Albert shook his head. Then he said, "You miss them, don't you?"

The days became almost a week. Albert started haying. The days were hot, steamy. Suzy came up one morning and sniffed at all the bushes, went to the back steps, whined. When I went out, she looked at me, questioning. Then she went and lay down in the side yard where Pat used to lie in the sun. She stayed almost an hour, then went back down the road, puzzled and dejected.

We went fishing again that evening. The perch were biting and we stayed out late. I heard the telephone ringing as we drew up at the dock, but it had stopped before I could get in the house. I went back and secured the boat, put on the cover, fileted the fish. Back in the house, the phone rang again.

It was Charley. "Out fishing?" he asked. There was a strange note in his voice.

"Just got back. Was it you who called a little while ago?"

"Yes. Want a dog?"

There was something in his voice, some exultant note, that made me ask, "What's his name?"

Charley laughed. "He's here!"

"No!"

"Yes! He got here about an hour ago. Thin as a rail and all worn out. I fed him and he's here in the kitchen asleep right now."

"I'll come up and get him."

"Better leave him here tonight."

"How did he act? Glad to be back?"

"Tickled to death. A little sheepish, but— Look, if old Pat wants to stay here—well, he's welcome. We're going to keep him here in the valley somehow!"

"Good! I'll see you in the morning, Charley."

I turned to Barbara. She had guessed, from my end of the conversation, what had happened. "He's back!" she exclaimed. "He came back!"

"Not to us," I reminded her. I felt let down.

"To Charley's, though! Back to the valley!"

The more I thought about it, the more I wondered. Where did Pat come from, anyway? Not this time, but originally, when he first came to us. He wasn't just a tramp dog. He had been raised in a good home, splendidly trained. He had a background. I had begun to forget that, he had become so much a part of our own household. Now I wondered why, when he was taken far off, to that New York farm, and ran away from there—he must have run away; why, I wondered, had he come back here to the valley instead of going back to his original home? If he was lost when he came here, surely he wasn't lost this time, when he came back. He could just as easily have gone somewhere else, couldn't he? Back to his original owner. If he could find his way back here, he could as easily have found his way to his earlier home. If not this time, then earlier, when he came here or any time during the past two years.

I couldn't find the answer. There didn't seem to be an answer. Charley had come up with the nearest thing to an answer when he called Pat "a notional dog." And that aroused a wry thought. Maybe he was all through with us. Maybe he had taken it into his notional head to stay with Charley.

I mentioned that to Barbara. "Maybe," she said.

And I said, "All right, if that's the way he wants it. Charley as much as said he'd be glad to keep Pat. And we wouldn't have to make arrangements for him when we have to go away on a trip." And I said, "I hope he decides to *stay* up there!"

She looked at me and smiled. "Oh, I'm sure you do!"

We called it a day, went to bed.

I got up the next morning, early as usual, and made the coffee and went into the library to have my first cup and read the daily newspaper. Yesterday's paper. It comes by mail, and I read it the next morning, having long ago broken myself of the habit of waiting impatiently for news that, if it is really important, can wait till I get to it. I sat there reading and sipping coffee, and about six o'clock I heard a sound on the porch. I looked over my shoulder, out the window.

There was Pat. Just getting up from his old rug in the corner of the porch. He got up, yawned, stretched, and glanced in the window at me. I exclaimed, "Pat!" and he wagged his tail tentatively.

I went to the door. He came slowly toward me, limping. He was stiff and sore, and his ribs showed beneath his dusty coat. He looked at me, questioning. I said, "Pat, you tramp!" and I held the door open for him.

He came inside, hesitant, as though wondering if he dared. I said, "Where have you been?" and he nosed my hand. Then he turned away and went into the living room and lay down on the rug in front of the Franklin stove. I went over and sat down beside him and he licked my hands. I looked at his paws. The pads were sore, worn and cut from travel. He licked them, one by one, then began licking himself clean.

Barbara heard us. She came to the head of the stairs and called, "Who's there at this time of day?"

"Who do you think?" I answered. "The prodigal!"

"Pat!" she cried, and she came hurrying down the stairs.

He got up to greet her, possibly reassured by my reception but more likely because he knew she would be more impulsive in her forgiveness than I had been. She exclaimed over him, rubbed his ears, then exclaimed, "Pat, you're dirty! And you always were such a clean dog! And you are half starved!" She turned to me. "Kill the fatted calf, then give him a bath."

I went to the pantry, got a can of dog food. She brought a second can and handed it to me. "You seem to think he's going to stay," I said as I opened them.

"Of course he is!"

I put the food in his pan at the back steps and came inside to watch from the window. He ate, went across the road for a few minutes, then came to the front door to be let in. He seemed to expect to fit into the old routine. I got a pail and a sponge and took him outside to give him a bath. He submitted with little complaint, as though this were one of the penalties he had come back to face. Then he rolled in the grass and came up onto the front steps and lay down to let the morning sun finish drying him.

Charley phoned a little later to ask if he was here. When I said yes, Charley sounded a little disappointed. "I let him out when I went out to milk, and next time I looked, he was gone. I figured he'd gone down to your place. At least to say hello. Well, I guess he'll stay around now."

That afternoon I phoned Dave, the dog warden. He had been expecting me to call, he said. Figured it would take Pat about this long to get home. The farmer over in York State had phoned him three days ago, said Pat had left there. Dave hadn't told me, not wanting to raise false hopes. "Seem to be settling down?" he finally asked. I said he seemed to be. "Nice dog," Dave said. "My little girl begged me to keep him. But I've got three dogs already!"

Pat lay around home, resting and healing his paws, for two days. Then he limped down the road after breakfast, visited Suzy for an hour, and came home. Before the week was out I heard the two of them battling a woodchuck in the lower pasture. And that evening when we went fishing, Pat went along. He prowled the riverbanks, swam the river twice, then hurried ahead when we turned back and was waiting at the dock to greet us.

The past was past. The incident of the disreputable little yellow bitch was all over and a closed chapter. Eventually he went up to visit Charley again, but Charley said he didn't go near the patch of alder brush down on the riverbank.

Pat didn't do much visiting, however, except to go down and see Suzy. He wanted to be near Barbara or me, though he was no more affectionate than he had ever been. When we were at our typewriters in the morning, he came to my study or lay at the head of the stairs, waiting for us to be through with this strange occupation, this peculiar tap-tap-tap thing we did. When we went out to work in the garden, he went along, to lie in the path just inside the gate and watch us. When we went to the village he watched us go, disappointed, and when we came back he danced to meet the car down the road, then barked his greeting and hurried to the porch to welcome us back, his people come home.

He loved to ride in the car, but somehow he knew that he was seldom welcome when the two of us went anywhere. When I went alone, he quietly and politely asked to go along, trotting beside me to the garage and waiting to be invited. If I said, "Come on," and opened the car door, he was in in a leap, sitting beside me and gravely watching the road. Unlike so many dogs, he never sat with his head out the window, ears flapping and tongue dripping. He was a dignified passenger, and he merely glanced at the dogs we passed, even when they barked at us. But the village was a place he had never explored, and it was full of interesting smells. He would happily have got out and taken inventory; but I raised the windows within a few inches of the top and told him to stay when I went about my business.

One afternoon I parked at the post office, tended to my business there, then went across the street to buy some office supplies. When I came back, there was no Pat. The windows were still up and I was sure he couldn't have crawled through the three-inch space above them. Then I saw that the ventilator panel on the driver's side was wide open. Somehow he had squeezed through there and got out.

I looked up and down the street. Not a dog in sight. I went to the corner, and still no dog. Had he taken off again? I started back to the car, and Morris, the foxhunter, hailed me. He was grinning. "Looking for Pat?" he asked. I said yes, and Morris said, "He's over in the next block. I saw him get out and watched to see what he'd do."

"Well, what did he do?"

Morris laughed. "He said to tell you he had to see a dog about a man and he'd be back in a few minutes."

I turned away to go look for him, but Morris said, "Give him five minutes. He said to tell you not to worry. . . . Seen any foxes lately?"

We talked foxes, and we talked fishing, and then I saw Morris look past me and smile. I turned and there was Pat, coming down the sidewalk, tail high and nonchalant. He went to the car and sat down and waited, and Morris said, "I told you. . . . Be seeing you when it's bird season!"

I went back to the car, opened the door, and Pat got in. He looked at Morris as I drove away, and something was said silently between them. Then he nosed my arm and looked up at me with a kind of dignified air of reassurance, practically saying, "You didn't think I wouldn't come back to the car, did you? After all, Boss, I would rather ride home than walk!"

July passed, and August. It was an early fall, frost the first week in September. One misty morning about the middle of the month I looked out and saw a doe and two fawns under an old apple tree in the pasture only a hundred yards from the house. They were eating windfalls. They were late fawns, still showing traces of their spots. It was almost nine o'clock and Pat had been down at Albert's on his morning visit for more than an hour. He should be on his way home. I stood at the window, watching for him, wondering what he would do when he saw the deer.

A few minutes later he came up the road. The doe saw him about the time I did. She turned and faced him, ears alert, and I heard her snort. The fawns hurried to her side. Pat must have heard too, for he stopped, looked at the deer, sniffed the air. Then he came on, trotting along the roadside uninterested. The doe watched him, moved a little way, the fawns at her flanks, then stopped to look again. Pat glanced at them again but came on toward the house. He passed within fifty yards of them and though the doe kept watching him she did not turn and run. Pat came across the lawn and up onto the front porch, and the doe and fawns went back to the windfalls.

Pat whined to be let in. I opened the door for him and stepped outside. The doe, with her sharp eyesight and uncanny hearing, must have seen and heard me, for she barked, spun around, flaunted that big white tail and galloped across the pasture. The fawns ran to her, then on ahead, their own white tails up and gleaming. I stood motionless, watching, and the doe stopped to look again. Then she uttered that barking snort once more, a sound almost like that of a gray fox, and she and the fawns went loping on across the pasture. They came to the fence and the doe paused while the fawns went over with their amazingly graceful leaps. Then she jumped the fence—actually, she seemed to glide over, it was so easy—and they disappeared in the brush.

The doe hadn't been afraid of Pat. Wary, but not frightened. When she saw me and perhaps got a whiff of my scent she knew it was time to go. And, even more important, Pat hadn't been interested in the doe or the fawns. I felt sure at last that Pat was not a deer-chaser.

October came and there were more windfalls under the apple trees. The deer came down to get them, seldom in daylight but almost every evening. When I went out to put Pat to bed I heard snorts and hurrying hoofs, and when I switched on my big flashlight I saw the dazzle of white tails as the deer fled, then the reddish gleam of their eyes as they stopped and turned to watch. It became a kind of game, to see how many deer I could count on any one evening.

Then one evening when I went out and there was the usual

rush, Pat sniffed a couple of times, yelped in excitement, and dashed off in the darkness. I couldn't believe it. I swung the flashlight and its beam picked up half a dozen deer still running, dashing toward the brush. I searched among them for Pat, but there was no sign of him. The deer reached the far fence, glided over and were gone. I swung the light here and there and finally saw Pat, beyond the big chicken house. As I put the light on him he began to circle and bark. Then I saw twin eyes close together, eyes the most beautiful ruby-red I ever saw. And the glint of a silvery pelt. Pat had something cornered. I hoped it wasn't a skunk.

I climbed the pasture fence, put on the light again. The red eyes were gone, but Pat was still dancing and barking. I ran toward him, and he dashed in, nosed something, stood baffled for a moment. Then I saw that my mysterious animal was an opossum. It lay there, inert, eyes closed, utterly limp, long ratlike tail not even twitching. Its coat was a grayish-yellow, which accounted for the silvery look in the light from a distance.

Pat nosed it again and looked at me, baffled. The possum's ruse was complete protection, at least as far as Pat was concerned. He didn't have to kill it. It was already dead. Or appeared to be dead. I have heard naturalists argue over what really happens when a possum does this. Some say it is nothing but an act. Others insist that the possum, faced with danger, actually faints, goes into a kind of coma. I am inclined to agree with the faint theory, for it seems to me that an opossum is so fundamentally incompetent, so ill-equipped for meeting a crisis, that its nervous system just quits at such times. Some biologist has reported that in this state the opossum's breathing almost stops and its heartbeat slows to a kind of quiver. Left alone for ten minutes, it catches its breath, its heart throbs again and it revives. This makes sense to me.

At any rate, this particular possum lay there as though dead, and Pat had no more interest in it. I decided to put him to bed, then come back and see what happened.

He went willingly enough. I closed and latched the door of his house and returned to the pasture. The possum was still there on the ground. I stood with the light on it and waited. Less than ten minutes after it had gone into its trance, or whatever it was,

I saw it catch a deep breath. Then it opened its eyes, lifted its head and looked around. It seemed unaware of the light. It got to its feet, looked around and trotted off toward the nearest apple tree. I followed it twenty yards or so away, keeping the light on it. Before it reached the apple tree it was busily searching for windfalls. It found one, took a bite, chewed it hastily and moved to another apple.

I followed that possum among the windfalls for fifteen minutes, and kept the full glare of the flashlight on it. It seemed totally unaware of the light or of me. It took bites out of fifteen or twenty apples, never more than two bites from the same apple, and it was soon scurrying as busily as a rat. Once it found what looked like a fat white grub and ate it, then went on sampling apples. And finally, for no reason that I could guess, it turned and hurried off into the tall grass and out of sight.

I never saw a possum among the windfalls again, and as far as I know Pat didn't either. But they are still around. Now and then during the summer I see one dead in the road, killed by a car. And every winter I see one or two, wallowing in the snow, looking bewildered and incompetent, eyes rheumy, pink noses sniffly, bare paws stiff with cold. I always want to say, "Why did you ever leave Virginia? What are you doing up here?" They don't belong here, but they persist, too stupid to know where they are, too fecund to die out.

Morris came over and hunted partridges. Pat greeted him happily, would have gone along—and been a nuisance—if he had been invited. Then the deep frost came, and November, and I went out with Pat to attend to the rabbits on the mountain.

For two weeks we went out for a few hours every other day. Pat would have run rabbits every day and all day if I had gone along, but I had other things to do, though the perfect fall weather made my study seem like a prison. Then it rained, one of those chill November rains, and we all were housebound for two days.

When it cleared again I decided to go with Pat far up the mountain and see if we couldn't put up one of those big white rabbits, the snowshoe hares. Pat didn't understand, though. Rabbits were rabbits. He put up three cottontails in the first hour and I got two of them, and we still were only halfway up the mountain. I hadn't the heart to put him on the leash. Then he put up a fourth rabbit, and instead of taking a stand I followed, hoping to intercept both rabbit and dog on up the mountain. The rabbit made a big circle to the left and ran in up there somewhere. Pat yelped his disappointment, then began to backtrack, looking for me. I finally shouted him to attention and he came to me. I let him rest, then went on.

We had gone another quarter of a mile and were in a stand of big white pines. Pat was up ahead, working the brush beyond. I came to a particularly fine pine and saw a littering of bark fragments at its foot. I examined one of the fragments. It was fresh-cut and had tooth marks on it. I looked up and saw a big white scar thirty feet up the trunk. Then I saw another scarred tree, and another. I had a porcupine, and he was already on his winter diet.

The porcupine eats leaves and field plants during the summer, turns to evergreen foliage in the fall, and in winter lives on inner bark of pines, hemlocks, sugar maples, even white birches. The worst of it is that porky wants only the bark from the best and biggest trees. He climbs to a comfortable perch, chips away the corky outer layers of bark, then settles down and gorges himself on the sweet cambium layer, the vital part of the tree. Often he girdles the tree, and though the tree may survive it dies from the girdled point upward. One big porcupine can play havoc in a grove.

The porcupine has few natural enemies, in this area. Disease, chiefly tularemia, afflicts the porky and probably is the ultimate control. But the lynx, the bobcat, the red fox and the fisher do the job more quickly where man hasn't cleaned them out as "predators." We have foxes and bobcats, but they apparently had overlooked this fellow who was working on my pines.

I forgot about rabbits and began watching the upper branches of the trees. I wanted to get that porcupine before he ruined every tree in that stand of pines.

Ten minutes later I was still there, searching for the criminal. Then I heard Pat. He was barking the alarm signal, in a shallow gully just beyond the pines. He barked and was silent. Then he barked angrily, a note I had never heard. Another silence. Then yelps of pain, followed by shrill, angry barking.

I ran toward the gully.

Pat was in the open, yelping frantically at a patch of low brush. He yelped, then stopped and pawed at his muzzle, then dashed toward the brush and yelped again. I shouted, and he turned and looked at me, and dashed toward the brush again. He had found the porcupine. His face was full of quills. Being Pat, he had attacked the porcupine, with the inevitable consequence.

I shouted, ordering him to come. He wouldn't leave off the attack. I caught him by the collar, dragged him away from the brush and snapped the leash on his collar. I tied him to a tree and went back to the brush. There was a papery rustling, then a grunting and the snapping of teeth. I circled the brush and there he was, one of the biggest porcupines I ever saw. He looked at me with angry, piglike eyes and lashed his tail. It made a rustly, rattly sound. Every quill on his body was erect. He looked big as a bear. I lifted the shotgun and fired, and he quivered and seemed to ease down on his side with a rustle of quills. He tried to get to his feet and I fired again. He lay still, the quills slowly folding down like foam subsiding. He became just another porcupine, a dead porky, but still an exceptionally big one.

Pat was yelping frantically. The shots had made him more determined than ever to get at this beast. I quieted him somewhat, and pulled what quills I could from his muzzle. Barbed as they were, they came out hard and painfully, Pat wincing and whining with pain. I got a dozen or more out of his face, and almost that many out of his lips. He was spitting, trying to get rid of those inside his mouth. He had really taken a mouthful. I opened his jaws and jerked another dozen quills out of his gums. But there were more, at least twenty, broken off short in his gums. I needed pliers or tweezers, or something, to get them.

I made sure the porcupine was dead, then started down the mountainside with Pat on the leash. He was still so full of fight and indignation that his hackles were up and I had to drag him the first hundred yards. Then he gave up on the porcupine. But, wounded as he was, his mouth drooling bloody saliva, he wanted to explore every brush patch. If anyone thinks it is an easy matter to lead a dog on a leash down such a mountainside, let him try it! Pat seldom chose the same side of a tree that I did, so I was weaving and backtracking all the way. And when a cottontail jumped from a form right in front of me, Pat yelped his trail cry and almost jerked me off my feet in his lunge to be after it.

It took almost an hour to get back to the house. There I got pliers and tweezers and went to work. Pat was patient, but I saw that the job was beyond me. I phoned the veterinarian, and he said, "Bring him over. We'll get them out."

I put Pat in the car and went over. The vet took one look and said, "He really got a mouthful! I'll have to knock him out with a shot and do a little operating. How about it, Pat?"

Pat was quivering on the table, tense but quiet. He must have been in considerable pain, and he was apprehensive. I held him and reassured him while the vet got his syringe. Pat winced at the needle but didn't make a sound. The vet said, "This will take fast," and he helped Pat down off the table. Pat looked at me with worried eyes. The vet said, "He'll still be a little groggy this evening, but you can get him after supper, if you want to." He started to lead Pat away. Pat staggered and stumbled, caught himself and stood there trembling. He whined at me, then gave up and followed the vet. I went back to the car, damning all porcupines.

Barbara, who had one look at Pat's mouth before I took him to the vet, didn't want to hear about either the vet or the porcupine. All she wanted was to have Pat home again, well and happy. I kept saying, "He's all right. It's just a simple operation."

"No operation is simple!" she said. "He could die on the table!"

"It's more like a dental job than an operation. Except that he won't have any teeth pulled, or even filled."

"You know how sick novocain makes me! Pat's human too!"

"He didn't get novocain. He got a general anesthetic."

"Gas or ether makes me even sicker!"

We waited through the afternoon, Barbara tense and jumpy. We sat down to supper. And the phone rang. Barbara answered it.

"Yes?" Her voice was taut. Then, "Oh!" It was a sigh. "He's all right? Oh, thank you! We'll be right over!"

We drove to the village, parked at the vet's office. I got out of the car, and a dog barked inside. Pat. I would know his voice anywhere. He had heard the car.

We went inside. The vet came to the inner door, greeted us, and went back. And here came Pat, wobbly on his feet, crying like a baby. He came to me, stood on his hind legs, thrust his head under my arm, and would have fallen if I hadn't caught him. He went to Barbara, nosed her hand, but remembered, groggy as he was, not to paw at her. Then he went to the door.

The vet laughed. "He didn't make a sound till you drove up. Then he began to cry. I took thirty-two quills out of his mouth. Thirty-two! He probably won't want to eat much for a day or two. His mouth's pretty sore. And don't worry if he's a little groggy. It'll wear off by morning."

In the car, on the front seat between us, Pat put his head first on Barbara, then on me, and he cried most of the way home. I had to help him up the steps at the house, he was so uncertain on his feet. He wanted nothing to eat, and he asked to be put to bed at eight o'clock.

The next morning he heard me coming to let him out. He barked impatiently, rolled in the frosty grass, dashed to the house and demanded breakfast at once. I fed him and we watched him start down the road, tail high, head up, good as ever and proud as a peacock. Barbara laughed. "You know where he's going, don't you? Down to tell Suzy all about his operation!"

CHAPTER 12

OUR AREA is not overrun by skunks, but we have our share of them. For the most part, they are good neighbors, making no demands except to be let alone. We let them alone, usually. When we don't, we are sorry and make firm new resolutions. Even Pat does. A skunk's spray is penetrating and incredibly persistent. But except in mating season, when the males wage bitter battles with every weapon they have, I have never known a skunk to make an unprovoked attack. All other creatures with any sense give them plenty of room. The only creature I know of that regularly kills skunks is the great horned owl, though a very hungry fox or bobcat sometimes kills and eats a skunk. I can't imagine ever being that hungry.

Skunks eat insects and all kinds of small animal vermin. They also eat an occasional bird, and if they get a chance they will raid chicken houses and become noxious nuisances. But one stray cat will kill more wild birds in a month than all the skunks that live on my place will kill in a season. So I have no quarrel with skunks, and I hope they continue to have none with me. Up to a point, Pat feels the same way. But he denies them the right to leftovers in his food pan and he thinks they should stay away from our compost heap. For a bright dog, Pat can be very stupid at times. Stupid, or stubborn—the result is the same when it involves skunks.

Most farm dogs have periodic encounters with skunks which, no matter what steps are taken, leave a reminder that asserts itself when the dog gets wet. I am quite sure I could tell you whether any dog had spent even a week on a farm during the past year if I were allowed to dunk him and then sniff.

The first time Pat swam the river I sniffed him while he was still wet. All he smelled of was river water, and I wondered at his history. He was an outdoor dog, definitely a country dog. Had he learned his lesson early? That was the only explanation I could find. Periodically I sniffed of him, and never did I get that rank, sulphurous smell of musk with an overtone of onions. At last I decided that he was really educated in this matter of skunks.

I don't know what happened to the skunks that winter. Maybe the hunting was poor, or maybe they decided to see how we felt about skunks. Anyway, they began to move in on us. The first sign of the invasion was harmless enough. I had fed Pat his supper and he had stayed out for a while. I heard him barking up on the mountainside a little way, probably at someone's stray hound. I went to the back door to call him in. I switched on the outside light and opened the door to step outside when some movement there caught my eye. I stopped and looked down. Right into the beady black eyes of a glistening black and white skunk not two feet away.

I froze where I was, scarcely even breathing. He stared at me for a long minute, then turned majestically and walked away. I waited till he was a full fifty feet away. Then I went on outdoors.

I found that Pat had left a part of his supper in the pan and the skunk had been cleaning up the leftovers when I interrupted him.

I switched on the flashlight and tried to see where he had gone, but he had disappeared in the tall grass of the pasture. So I shouted and whistled Pat in, and I watched where he came from. He didn't see the skunk and apparently he didn't get the scent until he reached the house. He sniffed his pan, bristled, growled, and was all ready to take off when I collared him. I brought him into the house and kept him here till bedtime, when I put a leash on him and took him out to his own house. It was well that I did, for as I started back to the house I turned the flashlight beam on the compost heap back of the woodshed and picked up a skunk busy there. He didn't like the light in his face and he ambled off in the darkness.

The next night I went out to look before I took Pat out. The skunk was at the compost heap again, and he still was in bad temper. I stayed my distance, but he backed around and warned me off, and his eyes glowed like orange-red coals in the light. Finally he left and I came around the woodshed. And there was another skunk, half again as big as the first one. I was within twenty feet of him before I saw him. But he was almost amiable. I focused the light on him and he sat up like a squirrel and folded his forepaws on his chest, and stared into the light. After a few minutes he got down on all fours and resumed his hunting. He wasn't a compost scavenger. He was after mice, and he caught two in the grass during the fifteen minutes I watched him.

For a week I watched the skunks with the flashlight. One night there were four of them, all within a hundred yards of the house. None of them really feared the light, though that bad-tempered fellow made his threatening gestures every night. I have heard that skunk spray is luminous in the dark, though I am skeptical. Chemically the stuff is n-butyl mercaptan, which is not normally luminous. It contains the hydrogen-sulphur compound which makes rotten eggs smell the way they do. I was tempted to toss a few sticks at the grumpy skunk and see if his spray did glow in the darkness. But somehow the experiment didn't seem worth while. I remembered the time when I, as a small boy, caught a skunk with a lariat. I thought the rope was plenty long, but it wasn't. And the skunk was very angry. Those who say a skunk can send a jet only ten feet or so have been misinformed. I don't know just how far a skunk can spray, but I know my mother made me bury my clothes, and she probably wished she could bury me for a few days, too. Anyway, I still don't know whether a skunk's spray is luminous or not.

I watched those skunks every night, and we became quite well acquainted. I didn't lose my respect for them, but I got careless. One evening I failed to put the leash on Pat before I let him out to go to his house. I opened the door for him, and he sniffed at his pan and took off like a cat with its tail on fire. A skunk had been at his leftovers only a few minutes before.

I ran after Pat, but he was around the woodshed in two jumps, barking like mad. Then he yelped in anger. And an instant later I knew what had happened, or thought I did. The clean, cool night air became tainted. Another breath and it became rank. Still another and it was neither clean nor cool but a thick cloud of sulphurous skunk spray. I didn't notice whether it glowed as I swung the flashlight beam here and there. All I saw was that Pat was over under the big apple tree, barking furiously, and that out in the edge of the pasture, fifty feet away, was a skunk, tail high, mincing along, taking his time and looking back repeatedly. His eyes were like points of angry fire.

I began to cough, and smothered the cough and shouted at Pat. He didn't need my warning. He stayed where he was, but he kept on barking threats and insults at the retreating skunk.

The air was heavy, rancid. A skunk has twin jets or nozzles at the base of its tail, each with its own scent gland. Each gland contains enough fluid for four or five charges. The jets can be discharged separately or together. That skunk must have fired both at once and emptied both glands.

I hurried out of the area of maximum contamination, calling Pat. He finally came to me, still bristling, still barking threats. Strangely, he didn't seem to smell any worse than the surrounding air. I put the light on him and looked at his eyes. They were no more than usually bloodshot. He hadn't taken the charge in the face. If he had he would still be rolling in the grass, writhing in agony, for skunk spray burns like fire and can cause temporary blindness. Somehow, Pat had provoked that skunk into using its weapons and still had avoided the direct blast.

I congratulated myself, and I congratulated Pat.

Then I heard the back door open. Barbara shouted, "Hal! There's a skunk!" And immediately the door slammed shut again.

I laughed. Her statement wasn't absurd; it was a gross *under*statement. Then I realized that the polluted air must already have begun to filter into the house. I ran to the door and opened it and called to her, "Don't open any windows! It'll be worse if you do." And she, from the kitchen, cried, "Close the door! Please!"

I went back to Pat. It didn't seem to me that he smelled too bad, certainly not bad enough to demand a bath that night. After all, the temperature was below freezing. So I took Pat to his house, let him in and latched the door.

I went back to the house, not realizing that my nose was virtually paralyzed by then. I went in the back door and into the kitchen. Barbara gasped. I knew, before she said a word, that I wasn't welcome. She gasped and gagged, and she managed to say, "You—you got skunked!"

I didn't try to explain. I went back outdoors. I reeked, and I knew it. Every stitch of clothes I had on was polluted. There was nothing to do but strip. I stripped, left all my clothes in a heap on the grass, and went in again.

Barbara had retreated to the bedroom upstairs. I went to the bathroom and tubbed myself with the strongest soap in the house. That helped, but it didn't really cleanse me. Barbara deserved a citation for heroism, and herewith gets it, for staying in the same room with me that night. That bedroom is on the river side of the house, away from the woodshed and the site of worst contamination, so we opened the windows wide. That sort of evened things off. The night air, even there, was still heavily tainted, and in a way it compensated for the odor that still clung to me.

It wasn't a good night for sleep. By morning, however, we had both made a kind of olfactory accommodation. The scent was still there, but we were less aware of it. Indoors, at least. Outdoors, in the back yard, even my insensitive nose recognized an unhealthy situation.

I went to Pat's house and opened the door. A wave of the skunk odor hit me in the face. Pat dashed outside, stinking to high heaven. Last night I couldn't smell him at all. This morning I couldn't have ignored him fifty yards away. He dashed happily to the apple tree and to the area where the skunk had let loose its charge. Even Pat recoiled there. He turned and walked away, bristling. He went to the back door, expecting to be let in.

I didn't even argue. I said, "No!" And I came inside, changed into the oldest clothes I owned, got a pail of warm water, put a handful of strong detergent in it, and got a big can of tomato juice. I went back out, cornered Pat, worked the tomato juice into every inch of his thick hair, then scrubbed him with the detergent and finally rinsed him twice with clean water. He shivered and I shook, for the temperature was down to twenty. I got an old bedspread from the woodshed and after he had shaken and rolled himself several times I dried him the best I could. Then we went in the house. Neither of us smelled like a rose, and Pat was a pink and black dog; but we were almost socially acceptable again. Almost.

It snowed that afternoon, thanks to merciful providence, and buried the skunk spray there in the back yard beneath a clean, white cover. But it was days before the house smelled normal. Or Pat either. Two months later we had guests in for dinner, and afterward, sitting in the living room before the open fire, someone began to sniff. "I'll bet," he said, "there's a skunk around here somewhere."

Barbara looked at me, and I looked at Pat, basking in front of the fire. I called him and sent him upstairs to my study. And we had to tell the guests the whole unhappy story.

It was during that time that we began to call Pat "Stinky." He seemed to recognize the name from the start, even to know something of what it connoted. At first he looked away in chagrin when we called him that, but in time he merely looked annoyed. We still call him Stinky on occasion, but now he knows that it either means he is to leave the room or that he is going to get a bath. He accepts the name with an air of resignation, much as he accepts the name "Dog." When I call him Dog he knows it means that he is not quite in disgrace but in something less than high favor. But all the names we call him vary in meaning with the inflection. He knows that even Stinky can have a humorous flavor. He almost smiles when it is spoken in the right tone. And he knows that I am kidding him if I call him Dog without an edge to my voice. Even his real name has variations. "Patso" is a fond name, and he almost preens at the sound of it. "Patrick" is a sternly formal name that goes with a firm order. "Patrick, go lie down! . . . Patrick, come here!"

After the Night When Pat Chased the Skunk I watched to see that no leftovers remained in Pat's pan. And we made sure that few edible meat scraps went into the compost. By removing the bait, we lured fewer skunks. And when the snows came and began to pile up we seemed to be rid of them entirely. But a few weeks later I noticed that Pat went, almost every day, to sniff at a gap in the lattice around the base of the front porch. I went and looked, but could see nothing important. I did think I caught a faint smell of skunk somewhere in that vicinity, but the skunk smell still persisted here and there about the place. After the first two snows I watched for tracks leading to or from that gap in the lattice and found none. I dismissed the matter from my mind.

Then, one January day, with a foot of snow on the ground and a snowstorm in full blast, Barbara looked out the window and exclaimed, "What's that?"

I came and looked and began to laugh. There in the snow in the side yard was a skunk, wallowing his way toward the pear tree beside the vegetable garden. He was having a hard time of it in the deep snow, his white-tipped tail waving from side to side like Pat's white tail-tip when he was swimming. He was plowing a furrow through the snow that all but hid him.

"A skunk?" Barbara asked.

"It certainly is!"

"What's he after?"

"Something to eat, probably."

In the winter we hang a cylindrical bird-feeder from one limb of the pear tree and keep it stocked with mixed seed. That year we had also hung a wire-mesh suet basket there. The suet basket hung a good five feet from the ground, but the skunk must have smelled it. He wallowed his way to the foot of the tree and sat up and looked at it, hungrily.

Suddenly the thought struck me. The skunk had come from

the house! I went out on the front porch and looked. Sure enough, the trail in the deep snow led from that gap in the lattice to the sidewalk that comes around the house, down the walk to the cellar door, then directly across the yard to the pear tree. Pat had been right all the time. We had a winter guest. That skunk had taken up cold-weather quarters under the porch.

Pat had sensed the excitement. He had been lying at the head of the stairs when I went out on the porch. Now I heard the storm door slam and turned and saw him there on the porch, about to bolt down the steps and into the yard. He saw me and hesitated just long enough for me to collar him. I hauled him back into the house and closed the inside door. Pat whined with excitement, clattered to the kitchen window with me.

The skunk had heard the door slam. He was wallowing back along his furrow in the snow, watching the house with anxious eyes. I went to the fishing closet, got down the shotgun from its pegs, thrust two shells into the breech. Pat began to bark, beside himself as always at the sight of a gun. I ordered him to go lie down, and I hurried out onto the porch again, closing the inner door behind me.

I went to the end of the porch. The skunk was still trying to hurry through the deep snow, back toward his haven. Then he was beside the cellar window on that side of the house, and he must have seen his own reflection in the glass. He sat back on his haunches and stared at it, baring his teeth. I shot him right there. He twitched, then lay still, and the stench of his spray, released in that final convulsion, began to fill the air.

I came back indoors. Pat was dancing and barking with excitement, demanding to be let outside, to get at the beast, whatever it was. He hadn't seen it. I managed to close the door and keep him inside, and I put the gun back on its rack.

Barbara said, "You got it?"

I said, "Yes. I'll let things settle out there a little while, then dispose of the carcass. He fired a farewell salute."

Barbara sniffed. "So I smell."

There was a faint taint in the air.

Then I heard the furnace go on. The house is heated by oil with forced-draft hot air, and the cold air I had let in with my trips to the porch had set off the thermostat. The furnace went on, and a few minutes later the blower went into action. The skunk smell became stronger. I went into the living rom. It was even stronger there. I went into the front hall and Pat, who had been sitting beside the hot-air register at the foot of the stairs looked at me accusingly and went upstairs.

Barbara called, "Are you sure you killed that skunk? It's getting worse!"

"Of course I killed it," I said. But I went to the basement door and opened it. A blast of skunk struck me in the face. I closed the door and went downstairs. The basement reeked.

Then I knew what had happened. I had shot the skunk just outside the south window to the basement. Its parting salute must have sprayed that window. The odor had seeped in around the window frame, and when the blower went on it sucked the odor right into the basement. Now it was blowing the stench all through the house.

I pulled a switch and stopped both the burner and the blower, and I went upstairs and told Barbara what had happened. She had begun opening windows, was struggling with storm sash. I put on a coat and went outside, got a shovel and took the dead skunk out into the pasture and buried it in the snow. Then I came back into the house. The fresh air was sweeping through, but the odor of skunk was everywhere. And the temperature indoors was swiftly sagging toward the outdoor level, which was around ten above zero.

I opened the door to the basement. It still reeked. Barbara found a spray-can of room deodorizer. I squirted it down the stairway. It helped a little, but not enough. I went down and squirted it all around that south window. Then I turned on the furnace and the blower again. Barbara shouted, "Turn it off! Quick! It's terrible up here when you turn it on!"

I went back upstairs. "The stuff must have saturated the air filters in the blower," I said.

"Can't you take them out?"

"I can, but—" I went over a list in my mind: vinegar, tomato juice, catsup. Then I asked, "Where's that awful Christmas perfume?" Someone full of good intentions had given Barbara a big bottle of synthetic gardenia perfume. Barbara loves gardenias, but there's something about gardenia perfume, especially the synthetic kind, that doesn't exactly delight our nostrils. This must have been double strength. Barbara had opened it, sniffed once, and put it far back on a high shelf in the bathroom closet.

"No!" she exclaimed. "Not that!"

"Would you rather have the place reek of skunk, or of gardenias?"

She got the bottle. I took it to the basement, removed the cover from the blower compartment, and drenched the air filters. I took the open bottle and splashed it all around the south window. I spattered it on the floor here and there. Then I turned on the switch once more. The furnace roared. The blower blew.

Barbara, at the head of the stairs, called down, "Still skunk!"

"Still blowing out the ducts," I said. "Give it another minute or two."

We waited. I poured the last of the perfume on the filters and replaced the cover on the blower.

"Here it comes!" Barbara finally shouted.

I went upstairs.

Did you ever smell the mingled fragrance of skunk and gardenia, both raised to the nth power? Then be thankful. It is like no other odor in this world, at once cloying and nauseating. But it is considerably better than the odor of skunk alone, particularly if the skunk odor is concentrated, heated, and blown at you in a blast from a hot-air furnace.

The furnace continued to roar and the blower blew, and we stood at an open window and breathed the clean, cold air and waited. And finally, after no more than twenty minutes, the perfume began to dominate. Half an hour and we closed all but two north windows.

"Did you use *all* that perfume?"

"Every drop."

"I was afraid so." She shook her head. "Well, we can have fried onions for supper."

"Onions? No, please, not *onions!*"

"No, I guess not. But something strong. Cabbage?"

"Let's try cabbage."

I heard Pat coming downstairs. He came into the living room and looked around, sniffing. He looked pleased. He sniffed, stood there a minute, then went into the front hallway and lay down, facing the hot-air register. I went to see what was going on. He had his nose within six inches of the register, and his nose was wriggling with pleasure. He breathed deeply, sighed, closed his eyes and went to sleep, an almost blissful look on his face.

I called Barbara. She came and looked. "That dog!" she exclaimed. "He loves gardenia perfume, and we never knew it!" Then she said, "Let's have sauerkraut instead of cabbage."

It wasn't the non sequitur it might appear. Pat also loves sauerkraut, though it took us a long time to find it out. For months we wondered why he came and stared hungrily into the kitchen every time Barbara cooked kraut. And why, when we had kraut for dinner he looked moodily at me when I gave him his routine dogfood dinner and then picked at it in obvious disappointment. We thought it was the smell of smoked meat, ham or hocks, that Barbara cooked with the kraut. He always got the bones and gnawed them happily, but he always seemed to be asking for something more. And finally I said, "Do you suppose he wants some of the sauerkraut *juice?*" Barbara said, "He's a most peculiar dog. He likes green beans and he eats spinach, sometimes. Maybe he likes sauerkraut juice."

I poured a cupful into his pan, and he lapped it eagerly and asked for more. I gave him the rest of the juice and the leftover kraut, and he licked up every drop and strand of it. Sauerkraut was one of his special treats. After that Barbara cooked an extra helping every time we had it, just for Pat.

His tastes are strange, and he still surprises us from time to time. Lobster, for instance. It seemed incredible that he should like lobster, but every time we boiled lobster he licked his chops and waited expectantly for a hand-out. He never got one. Lobster is no fare for a dog. We ate our lobster and put the empty shells with the trash in the woodshed to take to the dump. Then one day I left the woodshed door ajar and half an hour later I found Pat in the side yard with a litter of lobster shells around him. He had pushed the door open, salvaged the shells and was licking them clean. He looked at me guiltily, knowing he wasn't supposed to raid the trash. But ever since then he has had the privilege of licking out the lobster shells when we are through with them.

I still don't know all his peculiar tastes. He doesn't care for candy or any such sweets, but one day I caught him licking a discarded watermelon rind. Cheese, of course, is a treat, any kind of cheese, the riper the better. On occasion he will eat boiled onions. Baked Hubbard squash sometimes pleases him, but he has no use for summer squash. Carrots leave him cold, but boiled parsnips are a treat. In fact, his tastes are so unpredictable that he now gets all the table scraps, no matter how improbable they may seem as dog food. Barbara says he will eat anything with herbs in it, but that is an exaggeration. He doesn't care for dill. But he will eat sauerkraut every day in the week, and lick up every last scrap.

Barbara cooked sauerkraut that day, and by late afternoon the aura of synthetic gardenia began to abate, defeated by the kraut. We feasted, that evening, and so did Pat. Only in the basement, around that south window, was there any noticeable reminder of the skunk. It persisted for weeks.

We didn't have to fumigate the house again until March, when the skunks began to mate. Why the truculent males chose our dooryard as their battleground is a mystery to me, but they did. Twice their stench wakened us in the night, and once I went downstairs and watched the final round of a battle between two bloody and bedraggled skunks in the driveway out of the garage. They paid no attention to the flashlight beam as they staggered about, snapping, snarling, trying vainly to muster more ammunition for their exhausted spray guns. When I finally shouted at them they were both ready to call it quits. They staggered off in the pungent darkness. Fortunately there was an upriver wind that night, and when we opened the windows on the south side of the house the wind cleared and sweetened the air by morning. But the car, even inside the closed garage, had a noticeable aura for some time.

March passed, and April was almost gone, and I said confidently that the Year of the Skunks had passed. But I spoke too soon. The last week in April Barbara shouted from her study, "There's another one! Out by Pat's house!"

I hurried to look. She was as right as rain. There was a skunk sunning itself beside Pat's house. I looked again, and several pieces clicked into place. Then I went downstairs and got the shotgun.

The old brooder house where Pat sleeps was built on concrete piers with its floor about six inches above the ground. Originally the space beneath was boarded up, but over the years the boarding began to rot away. There were a number of gaps in it. The previous summer a cottontail rabbit decided to live under the house. In some mysterious way I shall never understand, this cottontail reached an agreement with Pat. Unless I was around, Pat never chased that rabbit. I saw that rabbit hopping about the lawn half a dozen times, Pat lying unconcerned not fifty feet away. But if I appeared, Pat put on a great show, sniffing, finding the scent, yelping loudly, and always ending up in the raspberry patch. He yelped and thrashed about, and came back to me and as much as said, "No rabbit, Boss." As I say, the whole thing was beyond me.

Then something happened. The rabbit must have broken the truce, for Pat went after it in earnest. He finally tried to dig his way underneath his own house to get at it. The rabbit took the hint and moved out, and I partly filled the hole Pat had dug.

I had thought there was a faint skunk odor around Pat's house for some time, but until that morning I didn't take it seriously. Now I knew. This skunk had taken up quarters under the brooder house, expected to bear her litter there. And it was almost time for her to give birth. She was sunning herself in the mouth of the hole Pat had dug. Pat fortunately was down at Albert's, on his morning visit with Suzy.

I took the shotgun and went out the back door and around the house, keeping a big lilac bush between us. I didn't know what to do, not wanting to kill her where she was and have her foul Pat's house. She solved the problem for me. She got to her feet, heavy with young, and ambled off, across the barnyard toward the big barn. I followed her. She went around the barn, searching the grass for grubs, and out into the pasture beyond. I shot her there.

I was sorry to have to kill her. But she broke the rules. I have never killed a skunk on this place that wasn't trying to set up residence where a skunk doesn't belong. As long as they don't try to live in with us, any of us, my truce with them holds good. Apparently Pat observes the same rules of armistice, for I have never known him to attack one or be skunked outside the limits of our private domain here in the dooryard.

I had the skunk buried by the time Pat came home. I took him out and showed him the place she had been sunning herself, and he sniffed and looked up at me and as much as said, "A skunk. So what? I knew she was there all the time."

Maybe he had a truce with her, too, as he did with the cottontail.

CHAPTER 13

I sometimes wish that Pat had a less vigorous sense of responsibility, or a more vigorous sense of self-preservation. Especially where armed men are involved, strange men. When it comes to strange dogs, Pat knows what he is doing, when to fight, when to bluff, and when to run. Usually he does.

There was the early fall afternoon when I was cutting down the stalks in the sweet-corn patch to give the late limas more light, and I heard a dog barking up on the mountain. A strange dog. Pat heard it too, and got up from the path where he had been watching me and looked and listened, his hackles lifted slightly. That was his mountain. What was a stranger doing up there? I said, "Skip it, Pat, Skip it. Just a stray hound." He glanced at me and wagged his tail once or twice in acknowledgment, then went out the garden gate and started across the pasture. I called to him to come back, and he hesitated, listened again, and went on.

I watched as he crossed to the foot of the mountain and stopped to bark a challenge. There was no answer. He strutted along the fence and scratched grass in that defiant he-dog gesture, and went into the brush. I went back to my corn-cutting. Being Pat, he had to go and see. He would be back in his own time.

A few minutes later I heard the strange hound again. Then I heard Pat, the challenge, the warning, the "get off my land" bark. Silence, then Pat's angry bark. And a defiant yelping from the stranger. I stopped and listened. This sounded like trouble. Another minute's silence. Then Pat's angry barks were followed by snarls, yelps and yowls. I couldn't be sure whether the yowls and yelps were Pat's or not, but the trouble I had feared was in progress. I put down the corn knife, came to the house and got the stout ash stick I use as a walking stick on the mountain. It makes a handy club, light but strong. And I started across the pasture.

The fight had subsided. Nothing but silence up there. But before I had gone fifty yards it was on again, this time among the trees just beyond the brush that lines the pasture fence. Most of the yowling was by the strange dog, I was glad to hear.

Then that ruckus ended. I hurried on.

I was halfway across the pasture when Pat burst from the brush, running full tilt. It wasn't like Pat to run that way. Then, ten yards or so behind him, a long-legged black hound crashed into sight, trying to catch Pat. Pat glanced back, saw that the black hound was gaining on him, and turned to face him. The black hound closed with Pat and Pat somehow knocked him off his feet, though the stranger must have been ten pounds heavier. Pat was on him in an instant, snapping at black legs and throat. He was winning the fight, but he glanced at the brush, then turned and ran again. And a big brindle dog, heavy-jawed and twice Pat's weight, burst from the brush and lumbered toward him.

So! This wasn't a row with another hound. This was a gang fight, and Pat was fighting a delaying action. The black hound could outrun him, but he could fight the black to a standstill. The big brindle was slow on his feet but he could have shaken Pat as Pat shakes a woodchuck.

Pat ran. The black hound scrambled to his feet and resumed the chase, the big brindle now almost at his shoulder. Pat was only two or three jumps ahead of them.

I yelled and ran to meet them, clubbing my walking stick and wishing I had brought a gun. Pat heard me and raced toward me, gasping for breath, long ears flying. I thought he was going to make it, but the black hound was too fast for him, even in the open pasture. The hound drew alongside, lunged at him, and they went over and over, a tangle of snapping jaws and raking paws, not twenty feet from me.

I thought Pat could take care of the black hound, for the moment anyway, if I could keep the big brindle from getting into it. He was closing fast. I yelled again and the brindle saw me and hesitated just long enough for me to get within reach and swing my club. I caught him alongside the head with it. He roared in pain and surprise, gathered himself to make a leap at me, and I brought the club down again, right across his muzzle. That took the fight out of him. He turned and I got in one more whack, across his rump. Then he was on his way.

Pat was on his feet, wallowing the black hound. But Pat had fought his fight. Fought his fight and run his race. He eased off, the hound squirmed to his feet, and I gave him one rap with the club. He yelped and scuttled away, saw the big brindle loping toward the road, looking back anxiously and shaking his head in pain. The black followed him.

Pat stood panting, exhausted. He looked up at me, wagged his tail and caught a deep breath. Then he trotted after the retreating enemy and barked, hoarse but defiant. He scratched grass. Then he came back to me and practically said, "Thanks, Boss. I guess we showed those tramps who owns this place!" And we came back to the house.

The black hound had bloodied one of Pat's ears a bit and he must have cracked a bone in Pat's left foreleg, because he limped painfully for two weeks. But except for that and a sore stiffness for a few days, he was unhurt. We never saw the black hound or the big brindle again. They must have been strays, for neither of them wore a license tag or a collar.

Then it was hunting season again, and Pat had other things than stray dogs to worry about.

Like almost any rural area, we have our troubles now and then with invading hunters. With poachers, too; but poachers are a special breed of outlaws. Pat is suspicious of invading hunters, but he hates poachers. How he distinguishes between them I don't know; but he does.

Rural and village hunters, as a rule, are careful, friendly folk who watch where they shoot, make sure of their kills, put up bars, close gates and are courteous people. It's the outsiders—

mostly from the urban areas, I am sorry to say—who cause the trouble.

One summer Saturday two affable strangers stopped at Charley's place and asked if they could hunt woodchucks. Charley was overrun by woodchucks that year, so he told these men he had cows up in the woods and he told them which fields they could hunt in and bade them good luck. They used up a lot of ammunition and reported that they had killed eight woodchucks. And they asked if they might come back the next weekend. Charley said all right. The next Saturday they came back with two friends, fired twice as much ammunition and had a noisy afternoon. After they had left Charley found two gates open, a broken whiskey bottle in the lane, and footpaths all through his best alfalfa. Charley didn't like it, naturally.

The next weekend they were back, this time seven men in two cars. They parked and began unloading arms and ammunition. Charley went out and told them the party was over. No more hunting, woodchucks or anything else, on his land. They wanted to argue. Charley said, "Get out." And he was abused in loud and vulgar language. But he sent them packing, then went out and put up more "No Hunting" signs.

The whole valley has been posted for some years, and that's the reason. The careful, courteous hunters suffer for the sins of the careless, arrogant minority. And we all take abuse for it.

One Saturday that fall I saw a station wagon cruising up the road. Pat, who was inside the house, announced that it had stopped here. I went to the door just as two of the four men in the car stomped onto the porch and announced, "We're going to hunt here. It's all right, isn't it?"

Pat bristled, and so did I. I grabbed Pat by the collar, and I said, "No, it's not all right. This land is posted."

The spokesman exclaimed, "Everything around here is posted! We buy hunting licenses, then you won't let us hunt! What kind of a deal is that?"

"There isn't any deal," I said. "I own this land, I pay the taxes, and I say no hunting here." And I closed the door.

They went back to the car and drove slowly up the road. I let Pat out. A little later they came back down the road, and soon after that Pat began to bark. I looked out and saw all four men, in their brand new gear, walking across the lower pasture toward the woods. I went out and shouted at them, and Pat ran toward them, barking. One of them lifted a gun and pointed it at Pat, and I shouted another warning. He lowered the gun, and they went on. I got out my car and drove down the road to where their station wagon was parked, out of sight of the house but within ten feet of a "No Hunting" sign. I followed them across the pasture. They waited at the edge of the woods, defiant. I didn't know whether they would threaten me with a gun, or shoot Pat, who was still barking angrily at them, or what, but I ordered them off. I had to tell them that my wife was calling the State Police—which turned out to be the truth—before they went back to their car and left the valley.

A couple of weeks later I was working in the yard when two rifle shots from up on the mountain crashed into the big barn not a hundred feet from the house. Pat went charging across the pasture, barking furiously, and I followed him, just as angry. Only a few hundred yards up in the woods we found two happy-go-lucky fools who said they were lost and had been shooting squirrels. With .30-30 rifles, no less! Guns that will kill a deer at a quarter of a mile or more. I made them unload their guns and I escorted them down here and back to their car, parked just up the road. Practically under a "No Hunting" sign.

Such hunters are nuisances. They are dangerous, usually, only because of ineptitude or carelessness. They are the reason for the "No Hunting" signs. But the poachers are something else again.

Connecticut has no open season on deer. A farmer, if he has a permit from the State Game Commission, may take deer on his own land, and he may apply for permits for his employees or close relatives to take a limited number of deer on his land. Beyond that, all deer hunting is illegal here. But there seems to be a year-round black market for venison in certain restaurants in nearby states. I am told that the going price at the moment is seventy-five dollars apiece for fresh-killed deer. So we have poachers.

The poachers usually work in teams of two men. Occasionally they make a kill in daylight, but usually they work at night. This calls for jack-lighting, a crime in itself; but the poacher is already an outlaw, so the added crime makes little difference to him. Deer are dazzled and briefly fascinated by a bright light thrown on them. Such a light is called a jack-light, though it may be only a big flashlight or even a car's headlights. Deer caught in such a light can be shot like sitting ducks.

A team of poachers cruises the back roads, usually at dusk, looking for roadside fields where the deer come down to feed. Having marked such deer meadows, the poachers return after dark, do their jack-lighting, kill a deer, drag it to the car, shove it in the trunk, and get away. If it's a deserted road with no occupied houses nearby, only game wardens or State Police can check the poachers.

If there are houses nearby or if the deer meadow is on a road where cars are passing from time to time, and if the poachers still want to take a deer there, one man may be left off with a gun and a flashlight, usually at dusk. He waits in the meadow for the deer to come down, and his partner drives away. When the deer appear, the man in the field jack-lights one, turns off his light and drags the carcass into hiding near the road. Eventually his partner comes back in the car. If the coast is clear he gets a signal, stops the car, helps load the carcass, and away they go.

Poachers hate dogs. And Pat hates poachers, as I said before, and he has some way of knowing poachers from ordinary hunters and from fishermen. Occasionally during late summer and fall fishermen drive up the road at dusk, park their car and go down to the river to fish for bullheads. When they have oil lanterns I know they are fishermen. But sometimes they use flashlights to see what they are doing and I mistake them for jack-lighters. Pat never makes such a mistake. He announces their coming and makes no more of it. But when a strange car, usually an old car with inadequate light on its license plates, comes drifting up the road at dusk, and Pat is suspicious, I know something is wrong. If he goes out into the road and looks and listens, then barks a warning, I usually go to the garage and get out the car. And unless Pat changes his mind I go up the road, watching for a parked car or a man in the field.

For some years now the State Troopers have been patrolling our valley road at night during the fall months, and last year the game wardens also patrolled it. All of us who live here watch for those suspicious cars and take down their license numbers, and if we hear shooting we phone each other, spread the alarm, and get busy. Last fall the Troopers and the wardens, with modest help from us, caught several jack-lighters. Fines running into the hundreds of dollars were levied and word seemed to get around to the outlaw fraternity. The poachers moved out. I hope we have discouraged them.

But during the fall I am writing about the poachers were still bold and there were quite a number of wandering hunters. Pat and I had a busy fall.

Usually when I feed Pat his evening meal he stays out no more than half an hour, then comes to the door and asks to be let in for the evening. But that fall he would be gone for an hour or more almost every evening. I would hear him at the foot of the mountain, barking, or up along the tracks, or in the Trestle Lot. It was his warning bark, his challenge, and I didn't like it.

A stub railroad track crosses my land, over which a few freight cars are hauled every other day. The track crosses the river on an old trestle and follows an embankment twenty or more feet high. Just beyond the embankment is what we call the Trestle Lot, a field that Charley farms. That year he had it in alfalfa, and the herd of deer on the ridge was coming down almost every evening to feed there or in my middle pasture. The embankment hides the Trestle Lot from my house, and it muffles the sound of gunfire. No other house is nearby or even within sight, so the Trestle Lot made a good field for the poachers to work. But the railroad track is also an easy short cut for hunters to take from the mountainside back to the road where they may have parked their cars. So I couldn't know whether Pat was challenging hunters or poachers. All I knew was that he was challenging someone who really shouldn't be there.

One evening he made so much of a fuss that I got into a heavy coat, took a flashlight and went out to see what was going on. He was up on the embankment just this side of the Trestle Lot. I cut across the back pasture toward him. Just as I passed the barn I saw a flash of light at the top of the embankment, saw Pat outlined in it. Then there was a gunshot. A bullet whined far over my head, a bullet that must have been fired at the embankment. The light went out. Pat barked even more angrily. Another shot was fired. It hit something and ricocheted with an even louder whine.

I shouted again and ran to the embankment. As I was climbing it I heard a car's motor start. I reached the top before I realized I would be silhouetted there against the sky. I crouched and held the flashlight at arm's length and turned it on the road. An old black car was just pulling away about two hundred yards from me. When my light caught it the driver gunned the motor and roared away without turning on the car lights.

Pat came to me, bristling, still barking at the vanishing car. I didn't know but what a poacher was still lying there in the frosty field, and I didn't care to have someone take a pot shot at me, so I held the flashlight as far away as I could and played it over the whole field. I couldn't find anything out of order. There were no deer there, of course. If Pat's barking hadn't put them to flight, the gunshots would have.

I put a leash on Pat and brought him home and called the Troopers. A prowl car arrived and I went with the Trooper and we searched the roadside for half a mile but found no trace of a deer carcass. "Your dog," the Trooper said, "scared off the deer, and the jack-lighters tried to scare him off, maybe to kill him. They won't be back tonight."

For almost a week I tethered Pat when I fed him, and I brought him into the house when he had finished eating. He didn't like the idea, but he accepted it. He would much rather have made his usual evening inspection. Meanwhile, the Troopers were patrolling the road every evening. And nothing happened. There weren't even any stray hunters walking down the track, and apparently the poachers were lying low or working elsewhere. The trouble seemed to be over.

I returned to the old routine, let Pat run after he had eaten. He was seldom gone even half an hour, and I thought everything had calmed down. Then, one evening when there was an overcast sky and an early dusk, Pat ate and vanished. I heard him once up by the tracks, barking. He barked only a few times, then was silent. But he didn't come back.

An hour passed. Barbara asked, "Where's Pat?" Not wanting to worry her, I said, "He'll be back pretty soon." She said, "He should have been back half an hour ago."

I went outside and called him. No answer. I came back in and said it wasn't really as late as it seemed, that the overcast made it seem darker than it was. Barbara looked at the clock.

We waited. An hour and a half passed. I was about to get my coat and the flashlight and go look for him when I heard him whining at the back door. It was a strange whine. I hurried to the door, put on the outside light. There he was, on three legs, shivering, barely able to stand. And there was a streak of red down his white chest.

I opened the door, had to help him up the steps. He got into the kitchen and almost fell down. He looked up at us with baffled, pleading eyes. He was hurt, badly hurt. I felt of his chest, pushed back the blood-soaked hair and found the wound just to one side of the center of his chest. It was no bigger than a lead pencil. He had sunk onto the floor and was breathing in deep gasps. But evidently whatever had hit him had missed his lungs. There was no bloody foam in his mouth or nose. I looked for another wound, where a bullet might have come out. There wasn't a second wound. I felt for his heartbeat. It was fast and fluttery.

"Do something!" Barbara cried. "We've got to do something! He's dying!"

I went to the phone, called the vet. "Bring him right over," he said.

"He's in pretty bad shape, may die on the way over."

"It'll take me as long to get there as you to get here, and I've got my equipment here. Bring him!"

I had to pick him up in my arms and carry him to the car. I drove much too fast, but I got him to the vet's office, carried him in.

"Put him over there," the vet said, "on the fluoroscope table."

He turned on the lights, searched with his eyes as he probed with his fingers. He listened with his stethoscope. "Heart's fast and irregular," he announced. "Only that one wound. Apparently no lung damage."

I knew all that.

"His left leg's paralyzed. Can't see a bullet anywhere. And only that one wound. Must have been either a small-caliber bullet or a spent one from a deer rifle."

Pat was so weak he just lay there. I had to pick him up to turn him so the vet could get another view.

"Apparently just missed his heart." He looked at me and shook his head. "Must have missed every other vital organ. His heart's beginning to quiet down, but it's still uneven." He got a probe, inserted it in the wound. Pat winced but made no other sign that he felt it. "Nothing there." He swabbed the wound with an antiseptic and reached for a syringe.

"What's that?" I asked.

He was loading it. "Adrenalin. A small shot may help. Unless there's an internal hemorrhage." He inserted the needle. Again Pat winced but he didn't object. The vet withdrew the needle. "I wouldn't do another thing at this point. We'll just hope he isn't hemorrhaging in there somewhere. He's a tough old dog and if he makes it through the night he should pull through." He went out and prepared a cage in the kennel room, then came back and took Pat in his arms and carried him out and put him gently in the cage. I went with him. Pat looked at me. His eyes seemed glazed, but when I put my hand on his head he tried to reach it with his tongue. I let him lick my hand. His tongue felt hot. He closed his eyes and sighed and lay back.

We went back to the vet's office. "What are his chances?" I asked.

The vet hesitated. "About fifty-fifty. You want the truth, don't you?" Then he said, "If you don't hear from me later this evening I'll call you in the morning."

I knew what he meant. I debated whether to take Pat back home and let him die there. Then I thought it would be better this way, no matter how the balance tilted, better for Pat, better for Barbara. Before I could change my mind I went out to my car and started home.

On the way home I remembered the time when they said I had only a fifty-fifty chance. Thanks to Barbara's faith and determination, my own stamina, and the skill of the doctors, I pulled through. Pat had the stamina, and Barbara and I had to have the faith. The vet had done all he could. If Pat didn't make it— but he would! I told myself that, firmly.

I told Barbara everything the vet had said except that fifty-fifty business. She was a little comforted, but all evening we both waited for the phone to ring. Waited, and hoped it would remain silent. When we went to bed at ten o'clock I told myself that Pat was winning the fight; he was still holding on.

I didn't sleep well. Maybe I was unconsciously listening for the phone that wouldn't have rung at midnight in any case. The vet had said he would call either during the evening or the next morning.

I was up at five, as usual, and made coffee, and tried to read. But I kept watching the clock. The second hand kept moving but the minute hand was awfully slow. The vet wouldn't call before seven, probably.

Barbara was up by six. She got her coffee and sat down and looked across the table at me. "I can't call before seven," I said.

She nodded, tried to read the newspaper, but I knew she was only glancing at the headlines. Finally she asked, "How old is he?"

"Eight. Maybe nine, maybe even ten."

"How do they figure a dog's age? I mean in relation to a man's age."

"Six or seven to one."

"That would be how much? I can't figure this early in the day."

"If he's nine, and if you figure six to one, that would be fifty-four. At seven to one it would be sixty-three."

"Middle-aged, at least." Then, "Oh, he can't be that old!"

It was full daylight. I watched the dawdling clock. We made toast. Barbara asked if I wanted bacon and eggs. No. I ate a slice of toast, just killing time. Then it was quarter of seven.

I went to the phone. I was about to pick it up when it rang. The vet's voice asked, "Did I get you up?"

"Been up two hours. How is he?"

"Come get him!"

"What?"

He laughed. "He just put away a whole can of dog food and he's out in the run right now, full of beans. Well, on his feet, anyway, and saying he doesn't want to stay here any longer."

"Well, thank the good Lord! I'll be right over."

In the car, Barbara said, "He didn't give him much chance last night, did he?"

"Fifty-fifty," I admitted. "How did you know?"

"It was written all over your face. But you didn't want to tell me. Or was it that you didn't want to put it into words?"

"Both."

We parked the car and went to the door. Pat began to bark, the greeting bark, somewhere out back. The vet let us in, and a moment later brought Pat. He wasn't really full of beans, and he cripped on three legs, that left foreleg still limp. But he hopped to us and whined happily. The vet said, "Frankly, I don't know how he did it. Tough dog. A lot of stamina." Then he said, "We'll have to wait and see about that leg. It's better than it was when you brought him in. That's a hopeful sign. He'll recover some use of it, I don't know how much." He gave me a tube of ointment for the wound and said he had given him a shot of penicillin. Then he leaned over and rubbed Pat's ears, wonder and admiration in his face.

Pat needed help to get in the car, but he sat there between us all the way home, quivering but determined in his own stubborn competence. I glanced at him and noticed, as never before, how grizzled he was getting around the muzzle, the frost of his years showing in his black hair, and I wondered how old he really was. Whatever his age, he was a tough citizen who didn't ask any favors of time.

At home, he made it up the porch steps alone and went into the living room and lay down in front of the fire. A little later he managed to climb the stairs and come into my study. But when he tried to go downstairs again he had trouble. I had to help him. He didn't come upstairs again for two weeks, until he could walk on that leg. It was several months before he lost the limp, but there was no permanent damage. Maybe the bullet grazed a bone in his shoulder and caused temporary paralysis, or it may have lodged there. Whatever it did, he overcame it and by the next summer could even run as well as ever.

The afternoon we brought him home I searched the pastures from end to end, looking for some clue to what happened. I couldn't find a thing, not even an empty cartridge. I still don't know who shot him, or why, or whether it was just an accident.

I wondered if it would make him gun-shy. Good hunting dogs have been ruined for the field by a stray shot or an accidental wound. I didn't go hunting that winter. It would have been cruel, with Pat still on three legs. But the first time I did take down a gun from the rack he was as eager and excited as ever, and the first time I fired a shot he leaped for joy and dashed to see what I had killed. In Pat's book, I never missed. I always wished I was as good a shot as he was sure I must be. Anyway, he certainly was not gun-shy.

But he was more than ever suspicious of all strange hunters, more angry at poachers and more jealous of these woods and pastures than ever before. Charley could hunt here, or Charley's grandson, George. Pat would run rabbits with them, happily. Albert could hunt here, though he seldom did. And Morris could hunt here if he came to the house first and Pat knew he was here. But if anyone else prowled the woods or the pastureland, Pat made a loud fuss and went personally to warn the trespasser off. And all strangers who came here, particularly at dusk or at night, got an angry challenge and a bristling threat that I wouldn't have cared to ignore.

CHAPTER 14

I N SOME WAYS, Pat mellowed with the years. In other ways, the years emphasized his whims. Sometimes it was hard to say whether the whimsicality or the mellowness was dominating. There were times when his headstrong notions seemed to verge on the eccentric.

One of his least expected whims appeared when we had to go down to the city for a week on business. Barbara told Ruth, Albert's wife, that we had to go, and Ruth suggested that we leave Pat with them. "He comes down to see Suzy every day anyway," Ruth said. "And he's welcome here any time. He's so well mannered he won't be any trouble. If he doesn't want to sleep in the house, he can sleep in the barn."

So we agreed. When we left we took him down there, with a week's supply of his own canned dog food. He seemed quite content and we went off without any worry about him.

When we returned we watched for him as we drove past Ruth's and Albert's. He wasn't in sight so we drove on, expecting to go back later and get him. But when we got within a quarter of a mile of our house, here came Pat to meet us. He watched till he was sure it was our car, then dashed happily to the garage to greet us when we got there. I got out and he leaped at me, whined, cried happily, then ran to the porch to bark his second welcome.

We opened the house, brought the bags in, and a little later Barbara phoned Ruth. "Pat decided he wasn't going to stay with us," Ruth said. "He went back home the second day. He wouldn't even come down here for meals, so we drove up there every night and gave him his supper in his own pan on the back steps. . . . No, he didn't object to us being there. He seemed to expect us to come and feed him. He was pleased as could be to see us, but he wouldn't come back with us. He did come down every morning to see Suzy, but he never stayed long. He seemed to be in a hurry to get home. I guess he decided he should stay there and take care of things till you got back."

That was the year we got a television set, but he didn't come home just to watch a TV program. I know that. Television never meant much to Pat. He accepted it, but I am sure he never believed in it.

After we got over the initial novelty I began watching Pat's reaction to the sound and the pictures there on the glass screen, particularly when animals were involved. One evening I turned on the "Lassie" program just to see how he would react to a dog on the screen. He lay there, facing the set, only casually interested. He watched the pictured dog for a few minutes, then closed his eyes and went to sleep. Even the televised sound of the dog barking made no impression on him. Then I changed to a blood-and-thunder program with volleys of gunfire. Again Pat paid no particular attention. It wasn't real gunfire, any more than the dog's barking was real, and he knew it. His ears were attuned to the sounds of reality, not make-believe.

One evening in the midst of a rather raucous program he lifted his head, listened, bristled, then went to the door and asked to be let out. I couldn't hear anything unusual, but when I let him out I went out onto the porch. There I heard a strange dog barking some distance away across the river. Pat had heard it in the closed living room, even with the television going. He went down to the riverbank, barked his challenge, then came back and resumed his nap and ignored those make-believe sounds coming from the television speaker.

Even though he had no real interest in television, he usually joined us when we watched it. He might be upstairs in my study, but when he heard the sound start he came down to the living room, apparently just to be with us. But that wasn't wholly new. He had always done the same thing when we used the record player.

But his reaction to the record player was different, probably because the player has a wider range of sound than the television speaker. I am sure this was a factor because he disliked certain records. For instance, a symphony orchestra playing Beethoven bothered him. I don't know why Beethoven, but he objected to almost any Beethoven composition. The same orchestra playing Brahms seemed to soothe him. He napped peacefully to the sound of Brahms, but Beethoven soon sent him out of the room.

Some popular music also annoyed him. When we first played the Broadway recording of *My Fair Lady* he walked out on "I Could Have Danced All Night," one of the best tunes in the show, though he didn't mind the loud hilarity of "The Rain in Spain." He accepted the blare of "Seventy-Six Trombones" in *The Music Man,* but he objected to the lovely "My White Knight" and "Good Night, My Someone."

Probably this was because of the overtones in certain soprano voices or in the orchestral accompaniment. A dog's range of hearing is different from that of a human being. It reaches into an area above the highest notes we can hear, into what we call the supersonic range, and there probably were painful overtones in some music. The "silent" dog-whistle uses this extra range in a dog's hearing.

Another aspect of Pat's night life at home appeared that winter when we wearied of television and resumed our reading aloud. For such reading we usually choose either Shakespeare or the classic Greek plays. That year we read the Greeks again. I am sure it was pure coincidence, but Pat walked out on Aeschylus time after time. I could read Euripides all evening, if my voice held out, and Pat stayed in the room without even a querulous sigh. It became a joke with us. "Pat," we would say, "doesn't like Aeschylus. He much prefers Euripides." And our friends would say, "So Pat is a literary dog?" Barbara would say, "In only a limited way. He doesn't write. But he is rather particular in what he wants read to him."

To tell the truth, Pat got restless when I read Shakespeare, too. Particularly if it was past his bedtime. But he never walked out of the room at eight o'clock when I was reading Shakespeare, and he did that repeatedly when I read Aeschylus. I don't know why.

All dogs like a regularity of schedule. Those who lay down rules in such matters say that dogs are creatures of habit, need a relatively fixed routine to be content. Until about that time there had been a degree of flexibility in Pat's habits and his insistence on routine, perhaps in part because he had been a kind of free agent before he came to live with us. But now he began to insist on a closer schedule. He didn't want to stay in his own house long after daylight. If I didn't let him out by six o'clock in the summer and seven o'clock in the winter he barked his impatience. Fifteen minutes' delay and he became insistent. I had previously given him his breakfast snack when I got around to it, between seven and nine o'clock in the morning. Now he decided he must have it half an hour after he got up. If I forgot it, he followed me around the house, reminding me. His big meal in the evening had been given to him any time between five and six o'clock. Now he set the time at five-fifteen in winter, six-fifteen in summer. If he didn't get it then he went to the kitchen door and waited with his "I am being abused" look. And nine o'clock, nine-fifteen at the latest, was his bedtime, company or no company. He made no secret of it.

Then an unusually warm summer descended on us, with hot nights as well as simmering days. Most summers we can count on a flow of cool air down off the mountain at sunset and usually there is a cool breeze coming up the river. But that summer the breeze failed us night after night, the mountain cool didn't come, and the days were hot and dry.

Pat never liked hot weather, not excessive heat. He endured it, but he preferred cold and snow. That summer he was particularly unhappy about it. When the day's heat began to build up around eleven o'clock in the morning he looked for some cool retreat. Sometimes he came indoors and lay in the hallway, where there might be a slight motion of air. More often he sought a shady green spot outdoors.

We have a large bed of lilies-of-the-valley under the pear tree beside the vegetable garden. It is shaded much of the day and that year the lilies were particularly lush, for some reason. Pat chose that for his retreat. The lilies-of-the-valley didn't appreciate it, and neither did Barbara, who loves lilies-of-the-valley. There was an argument that lasted two weeks, day after day, and I finally had to put up a low fence to persuade Pat that he wasn't welcome there. Deprived of the lily bed, Pat just disappeared for hours each day. It was a week before we found that he had made a hide-out among the big ostrich ferns that grow in a bed beside the house and in the shade of the Norway spruce. He was chagrined when we discovered his secret cool place at last. So chagrined that he still was sheepish about going there even after we told him it was all right.

The ferns provided some relief from the hot days, but the warm nights were still a burden to him. He became more and more reluctant to go to his own house at bedtime, even though all four windows were opened wide. One warm evening when we started for his house he turned and came up onto the front porch and lay down in a corner where there was a slight breath of air stirring. He said as plainly as he could that he wanted to sleep there. I don't like to let a dog of mine run loose at night. The darkness seems to invite a dog to wander and to bark, and a barking dog under my window or just down the road at night particularly annoys me. I am sure others feel the same way, so I like to keep my dog at home. But that was a summer to break the rules. I let Pat sleep out on the porch.

He probably would have stayed at home on those hot nights, thankful to be there on the open porch, if it hadn't been for the strange dogs that were wandering the valley that summer. I saw them only once, but I heard them from time to time in the darkness up on the mountain. The dogs I saw were big, rangy, rough-coated hounds that I couldn't identify as belonging to anyone I knew. One night they came down into the home pasture and barked, and Pat answered them, and there was so much of a to-do that I got up, pulled on my pants, went out into the pasture and shouted Pat in. When he came I put him in his own house and latched the door, heat or no heat. The next day the weather eased a bit and I housed him every night for a week.

But the cool spell passed and hot nights returned. I hadn't heard the strange hounds since that night in the pasture, so I relented when Pat tried to tell me he wanted to sleep on the porch again. I let him go out there, saw him settle down, and I went to bed. Once during the night I thought I heard dogs barking down the valley, and I listened for Pat's voice. I didn't hear it, and I went back to sleep.

I was up before five as usual the next morning. I made the coffee and sat down to read. I thought of Pat and the night's barking and I glanced out the window. Pat was lying in his corner of the porch, deep in early morning shadow. I went back to my reading.

Six o'clock and Barbara was up. She got her coffee and sat down and sipped it and asked, "Where's Pat?" He usually asked to be let in about the time she came downstairs. I pointed out the window and she glanced at him and asked, "Did you hear those dogs last night?" I said yes, down the valley. "They made a lot of noise," she said. "I thought it sounded like a fight. Thank goodness Pat wasn't in it." I said yes, apparently he had been home all night.

Seven o'clock and Pat still didn't come to the door. We had breakfast and discussed the work we planned to do that day, and I came upstairs to my study and went to work. Barbara went to her study. It was nine o'clock before I went downstairs again, to get another cup of coffee. As I passed the window I glanced out and saw that Pat was still there in the corner of the porch, still sleeping. That wasn't natural.

I went to the door and spoke to him. He opened his eyes but didn't move. I went outside and spoke to him again and he lifted his head wearily and tried to wag his tail. Something was wrong. I went over to him, there in the deep shadow, and saw for the first time that he was streaked with dust and blood. He sat up, painfully, and I saw that both his ears were wet with blood still oozing. There was a deep gash in his right shoulder and his neck was so swollen that his collar seemed to be choking him. I unbuckled the collar. It was gashed and chewed almost in two. It wasn't a broad collar or particularly heavy, but it must have saved his life. It had somewhat protected his throat. And I found that his right ear was a bloody mess already so swollen that it was an inch thick. His left foreleg, the one that always seemed to get hurt, was too sore to put his weight on.

Pat had taken a whale of a beating.

I let him lie down again and came in and told Barbara that Pat was hurt, apparently had been in that fight we heard. "Badly hurt?" she asked. I didn't answer her question. "I'm going to take him over to the vet," I said. I phoned, and the vet said, "Bring him along. I guess he knows this place by now."

When I went outside again Pat seemed to know where we were going. He got painfully to his feet and tried to go down the steps. I had to help him. He hopped on three good legs to the garage and waited for me to help him into the car. We drove to the village.

The vet put him on the table and went over him, looking for broken bones. There weren't any, fortunately. That left leg had been chewed up, had a dozen tooth punctures. The gash on his shoulder was deep, almost to the bone. The vet clipped the hair around it, salved the wound and gave him a shot of penicillin. But the worst damage was to that right ear, the good ear, the one without the slit. There had been a hemorrhage in it and it was full of blood. The vet said there was nothing to do for it except wait and see if it absorbed. If it didn't, within a week or two, he would have to operate. Meanwhile, better leave him at the vet's overnight. They would give him a medicated bath, patch him up all they could, and see if he shot a temperature.

Finally the vet stood back and shook his head. "Pat," he said, "don't you know that an old dog like you ought to stay out of gang fights? If you weren't so confounded tough—" Pat turned a bleary eye at him and gave him one look, and the vet laughed. "O.K.," he said, and he lifted him down from the table and led him away.

The vet phoned me the next morning. "Come get him. No temp. And he wants to go home."

So I went and got him. The vet said to watch that ear and to watch the wound in his shoulder. "He'll be sore and full of groans for a week or so, but if no infection sets in he should come around all right." He turned to Pat. "You'd better stay out of rows like that, Pat. You don't own that whole valley, do you?"

"Yes," I said, "he does. And he takes it seriously."

I brought him home. I hadn't let Barbara see the extent of his wounds the day before. Now she was appalled. That right ear looked like a thick slab of raw liver. His throat was still so swollen that his collar wouldn't have reached around it. The clipped hair emphasized the length and depth of the gash on his shoulder. She almost cried. Pat gravely accepted her sympathy, ate sparingly, and slept most of the day, as though knowing that time and his own stout constitution would have to repair the damage.

I stopped at Albert's that afternoon, wondering if Suzy or Cubby had been in the fight. Cubby was a gangling black and white pup about six months old that Albert had got a few weeks before. No, Albert said, Suzy and Cubby were where they always slept. They weren't in the fight. There were two fights, actually, or two parts of the same fight, and both of them sounded pretty rough. He had thought he heard Pat once or twice, but decided it couldn't be Pat, since he must be at home in his own house.

The first fight was in the little field across the road from Albert's house. It began about midnight and was a very noisy row. Albert finally got up, took a flashlight and went down to see what was going on. Nobody could sleep with all that noise. As he approached, the dogs broke off the fight and scattered in the darkness. Albert went back to bed. Half an hour later the fight started again in the driveway out by his barn. That one was less noisy and it ended in what sounded like a chase up the valley, toward my place. Then things quieted down.

"I had no idea Pat was in it," Albert said. "But we wondered why he didn't come down to see Suzy yesterday or today." He thought four or five dogs were involved in the fights. "Probably those strays that have been prowling the valley every now and then." And we agreed that if they stayed around we would have to do something.

As it turned out, they didn't stay. We didn't see them again that summer, and we didn't hear them on the mountain. I am sure Pat didn't win the fight. The odds were too great, and he took too much of a beating to have been the victor. But he may have given almost as good as he took. I'm sure they knew they had been in a fight. And I doubt that they wanted another encounter.

Pat lay around home four days, and he went willingly to his house every night. He didn't develop any noticeable fever, the wound in his shoulder began to heal from beneath, and though that ear was still as thick as my thumb it, too, began to heal. And Pat began to get restless, tired of being an invalid.

On the fifth morning he set off down the road, cripping along on three good legs. But his tail was high and he sniffed the air with something of his old eager assurance. I watched him out of sight around the first bend in the road, and Barbara said, "He's going down to tell Suzy all about it."

He was gone almost an hour. Then he came limping back and lay in the sun on the front steps, tired out. But the next morning he went to see Suzy again, and within another week he was using that injured leg, limping but using it. And not long after that I saw that his ear was better. The swelling had begun to go down and he could shake his head without wincing at the pain.

I had wondered if the beating he took would take the heart out of him, leave him an old dog broken in spirit. It didn't. Even before he lost the limp, he and Suzy were out after woodchucks again. And he was just as truculent as ever about his ownership of this place. Strangers, men or dogs, were challenged as usual.

Any lingering doubt I had was put to rest the day Albert came up to get a load of bedding straw from my big barn.

Both Suzy and Cubby, the pup, came along. Cubby was going to be a big dog. He was bigger than Pat by then, and still growing. He was a friendly dog, and Albert had said there never was any trouble between him and Pat down at his place. But this time Cubby was up here, at Pat's place. And Suzy was here, too.

I was talking with Albert and all three dogs were there in the barnyard, Pat was being very proprietary. Suzy was being coy; after all, Suzy was a girl, and here were two man-dogs. Cubby was young and naturally brash. Before we knew what was happening, Cubby called Pat a name or two, Pat bristled and growled, Cubby made a pass at him. Pat snarled and went into action. A noisy row was on in an instant.

Albert shouted at them, and I shouted. We slapped at them, finally grabbed them and hauled them apart. The minute we let go they were back at it. We hauled them apart again and I put Pat in his house and latched the door. Albert put Cubby in the cab of his truck. I apologized for Pat, but Albert said, "It's Pat's place. He was just trying to make Cubby admit it."

He finished loading the truckload of straw. Before he left he turned to me with a frown. "I don't know what to do about Suzy."

"Suzy?"

He nodded. "She's getting snappish, and she's causing trouble." He opened the cab door, let Cubby out. He started to say something more, then changed his mind. He didn't want to talk about it. He got in and drove down the road, Suzy and Cubby trotting beside the truck.

A couple of weeks later I saw Pat come home one morning within ten minutes after he had started down to see Suzy. I watched him come up the road, stopping from time to time to turn and look back. He came into the yard and lay down in the grass, but he didn't nap. He lay there, looking down the road as though baffled. The next day the same thing happened, the trip down, the quick return, the baffled look. Something was wrong. Something was out of place in his world.

I saw Albert, and before I could ask him he said, "I had to get rid of Suzy."

"She's gone?"

"Put her away." He sighed. "I guess old Pat can't understand what happened. He comes down and looks around and whines at the door, and then he leaves."

"I wondered. So that's it."

He nodded, and I didn't press him for details.

For ten days Pat continued to go down there every morning, look for Suzy, and come back home. And he seemed to draw into himself, somehow, as though in a kind of puzzled mourning. Then he stopped going. He would go out and look down the road, stand there looking, much as he had when we sent Mike away. Then he would come back and lie down, not to nap, but to wait. He didn't want to go along when we went fishing. If we asked him, he would go with us on an afternoon walk, but he didn't prowl the roadsides and he was always eager to get home, as though waiting for someone, expecting someone. The zest for life seemed to have gone out of him.

"I don't like it," Barbara said. "He's a sick dog."

"He's a lonely dog," I said. "He misses Suzy."

"I think he's sick."

I took him to the vet. The vet checked him from nose to tail-tip. "Not a thing wrong," he finally said. "That shoulder's all healed, he's absorbed almost all that big clot in his ear, and his leg's all right. His heart's as good as it ever was. He isn't a pup any more, but who is? What are you worrying about?"

I told him about Suzy.

"That's your answer," he said. "He misses her. He's mourning for her, the same way he'd mourn for you if you turned up missing some morning. Sometimes a dog will mourn for months, even refuse to eat."

"Pat still eats."

He smiled. "So I see. He's getting a little overweight. Lack of exercise, now that he's not running with Suzy. I'd cut down a little on his ration. I don't know what else to suggest. He's in good shape, physically. Teeth are still good, eyes are clear, and his hearing's all right. He could live quite a while yet."

I brought Pat home and told Barbara what the vet had said. "So," she said, "we wait for him to get things in place again. Is that it?" She turned to Pat. "Don't you know that we understand, Pat? Don't you know that *we* love you?"

Pat was lying on the rug, staring into space. He looked up at her, then turned away and sighed and lay back, disinterested.

He was napping in my study that night at bedtime. I went to the foot of the stairs and called, but he didn't come. I came upstairs, and he got wearily to his feet, went to the head of the stairs and stood there. I ordered him to go down. He took two steps and hesitated. I ordered again. He took another step and looked at me as though afraid to go on down. I had to take him by the scruff of the neck and help him down, step by step. I took him outside and he nosed the air once, then trotted wearily to his house.

The next afternoon I called to him and started off across the pasture toward the mountain to see what would happen. I had to call him twice before he followed me, obedient but without any spirit. He followed me across the pasture, at my heels. At the far fence he looked at me as though asking, "Haven't we gone far enough?" I crawled through the fence and started up the mountainside. I called, and he came along. He brightened a little in the scattered woods, and when he got a rabbit scent he yelped a few times and started to follow it. But after a hundred yards or so he gave up and came back to me. I let him rest a few minutes, then went on. But it was no use. He wasn't interested in the mountainside. I came back home, and he lay down again in the yard.

I didn't know what to do. That whole pack of stray hounds hadn't been able to break his spirit, though they mauled and chewed him unmercifully. But when Suzy went out of his life, Suzy, the spayed bitch from down the road, he became an old, dispirited shell of himself. The Pat I had known seemed to be dead.

I didn't like it either.

CHAPTER 15

CHARLEY stopped past and told me quietly that he had had to have Poochy put away. Then he looked at Pat and said old Pat was showing his age and wondered cautiously if he would last out the winter. "Wheeze much?" he asked. "Poochy did, toward the end. Some kind of asthma, or something." And Albert stopped in and said, "I wonder if that fight with the hounds took too much out of old Pat. Maybe it broke his spirit, getting chewed up that way." Then he added. "But he's no pup, after all. They get old."

September passed. No, that's not true. September never "passes," here in the Berkshire hills. September comes and lives among us, unpredictably fretful or placid, benevolent or tantrumatic, and altogether winsome. Even the occasional whiplash of an errant hurricane can't spoil September; it is human nature to cherish first-hand tales of devastation and disaster, and some Septembers have been both disastrous and devastating in New England. But when the hurricanes hold to their usual course, as they did that year, and leave our scarred hills to the mercy of less impatient elements, September is bounty and beauty, gold of goldenrod and purple of big New England asters. It isn't October but, until October comes to dwell here and make us doubt the Puritan denial of grace to the warm-hearted and the warm-blooded, September suffices.

Pat mourned and languished, but September came and dwelt on Tom's Mountain and here in the valley, and we picked and shelled the last crop of limas and picked the peppers, cherishing those that had outrun the season and turned red as Southwestern chiles. We debated whether to bring in the butternut squash and the acorns or leave them hiding among the weeds until the first hard frost had blackened the tomato vines. September is always a time of debate, not so much from conviction as from temptation. When the sky is blue and deep we believe that fall will last till Christmas. When the sky turns surly and the wind comes down the valley with a stinger in its tail we put on windbreakers and corduroys and dig carrots and late onions and pick half-ripe tomatoes to squirrel away in the root cellar. And I wonder if the woodshed is sufficiently stowed for the long, cold nights. Then the stinger-wind passes and the sky is blue again. I dig worms. Barbara fetches the rods. We go out for a little fishing and a lot of looking and listening and just plain sensing. We leave the garden's hostages to chance.

The blue-sky days came, that fall, and we went fishing and sensing. And Pat stayed home. For the first time, September meant nothing to him. It would have been easier, we told ourselves, if he hadn't survived the battle with the hounds. Easier for us and probably easier for him. Grief and loneliness are grim companions, especially in the graying years of life. As Albert had said, Pat was no pup. "They get old."

Then October came, with chilly nights and brisk days. I couldn't stay indoors. I had to go and see the purpling of viburnum leaves and the deep flame of the cardinal flower and the lacquered scarlet of the jack-in-the-pulpit's berry clusters. So I went, and Pat went part way up the mountainside with me, then turned and came back to the house, not even once yelping a rabbit scent. I went on alone, telling myself it didn't matter, it didn't matter at all. Dogs grow old, as men grow old, and Pat grew old before I did, being destined to a different time scale. For one reason or another, and the reasons are often obscure even to the one involved, life loses its savor. Man tames the beasts and links them to his own way of life, robbing them of the anodyne of fanged or taloned death before their prime has wasted into mere existence. Pat was old and life had become a full belly and a long nap and a gnawing emptiness of grief for something he couldn't even understand. What did it matter?

But it mattered a great deal, and I knew it. Omnipotent man that I believed myself to be, in that empty human arrogance, there wasn't a thing I could do about it. Except, when the time came, to take him to the vet and say, "Put him away. I haven't got the guts or the humanity to do it myself."

I wandered the mountainside, deep in the showering gold of maple and ash and birch, and I watched the squirrels choose unerringly the meaty butternuts from the meatless ones, and I was startled by the *brrrrooom*-ing of the partridges. I saw these things, and I came home to write down what I had seen and heard; but not what I felt, for the feeling wasn't there. Don't ask me why. It wasn't Pat. It was me.

Then, one mid-October day, I was here in my study, at the typewriter, trying to capture the feeling that wasn't in me, and I got up and went to the west window to stretch my legs and ease my eyes. Pat was here on the rug, and I stepped over him, and he didn't even seem to notice. I went to the window and looked out across the pasture, and a movement caught my eye. Up there near the Resting Rock, that fragment of weathered ledge that reveals the nature of the mountain's skeleton, old Gramp was out and feeding. Gramp was the big woodchuck that for a number of years had defied both Pat and me, as well as the natural hazards to woodchuck longevity. He was out there putting on that final layer of fat which would warm and nourish his minor flame of life during hibernation.

Maybe it was some inner need to vent my simmering anger, or maybe it was just the human blood-lust. I don't know what. But I turned and hurried down the stairs to get a rifle. I went into the fishing-pantry and lifted the gun from its high pegs, and I heard the click of Pat's claws in the hallway. He had somehow sensed my purpose and he had hurried down the stairs, scrambled on the bare floor, and now was whining toward me, ears alert, tail high. He saw the gun and leaped and dashed toward the doorway.

For a moment, as I made sure there were cartridges in the rifle's magazine, I cursed inwardly at him. Dratted dog got all excited at the sight of a gun. Wanted to get out the door ahead of me and yelp and bark and tear off in circles in the pasture and tell everything in sight that I was coming with a deadly weapon. Damn! Pat was a nuisance, always had been, that way. Have to keep him in, latch the door behind me.

Then, on my way to the door, it struck me. Why, Pat was Pat! He was himself again! Thank the all-wise Lord!

I let him out ahead of me, not caring whether I got a shot at old Gramp or not. I let him out and he leaped and barked and dashed ahead of me around the house. I got one look at old Gramp, on his haunches staring at me a hundred and fifty yards off; then he was just a brown scurry in the tall grass, making for his den among the rocks in the edge of the brush.

I took one snap-shot in Gramp's direction, more for Pat's benefit than anything else. Pat yelped happily and dashed out across the pasture. I followed, urging him on.

Pat found the scent before I caught up. He found where old Gramp had been feeding, nosed here and there, yelping frantically, and finally traced it to the den. He tried to dig his way in, was balked by the rocks, but scratched away and sniffed and barked and challenged and defied.

I stood and watched, fascinated. This wasn't Old Pat. This was Pat in his prime, Pat, the scourge of all the woodchucks in Weatogue Valley.

We spent twenty minutes there, and when we came back to the house Pat was puffing and tired, but his tail was high, his ears alert, his eyes gleaming. He licked my hand when I patted and praised him, and when we came inside he went to Barbara and practically demanded her praise, too. This was something entirely new. Then he turned away, seemingly abashed at his own exuberance, and lay down and licked his paws and pretended a blasé taciturnity.

That evening he came down the stairs when I summoned him, stiff but confident. When we went outdoors he sniffed the air, watched the mountain with alert eagerness and barked a time or two at some mysterious presence there or perhaps only at the starlight. The next morning when I let him out he rolled in the frost-crisp grass as he hadn't done in weeks, and he got up and looked up and down the valley and went off to explore the state of the world. *His* world. He was gone almost an hour before he came back and demanded his breakfast.

That was the turning point.

He ran the mountain with me again that fall, coursing rabbits. He hadn't quite the stamina he used to have, and now and then he lost a scent and came back to me looking chagrined. Sometimes he seemed to say, "I don't know what's happened, Boss. Those rabbits haven't as much scent as they used to have." And I tried to tell him they weren't as big as they used to be, either, and that my shotgun seemed to shoot a smaller pattern. I wished I had some way of telling him that it happens to all of us, that we wonder why people don't speak as clearly as they used to, and why they are using smaller type in the newspapers than they did ten or fifteen years ago.

But Pat put up his share of rabbits, and I shot my share. And we had those magnificent November and early December days when the sky was distant cobalt and the oak leaves were Burgundy and the brooks were liquid laughter. The woods were ours again, the whole mountainside, the whole world of our valley. When the snow came, before it got too deep, I told him, we would go far up the mountain and see about those big white rabbits. Life was good. Pat knew that again.

But other changes, subtler ones, had been going on in Pat. Barbara saw them first. When I went to the village on an errand, he insisted on going outdoors to watch me go. Then he would wait on the porch, watching the road. If I was gone more than an hour he would begin to whine. He would demand that Barbara let him in the house, and once indoors he as much as asked her why I was gone so long. He was restless, wanting out, wanting in again. Then he would hear my car far down the road and begin to whine happily, and hurry to the door and want out. He would come to meet me, as though I had been away for days, and he would accompany me into the house, demanding my attention, my greeting, a touch of my hand. Then he would settle down, content. And if we both went and were gone even half a day, he came to meet us far down the road, raced to the garage to greet us when we arrived, and was beside himself with pleasure at our return. His people.

I noticed a new and more open fondness for Barbara. I was still his man, but now she was his woman. She had been my woman, and Pat liked her and protected her; but the relationship was through me. Now it was independent of me. He wanted her affection, needed it, somehow. And got it. She talked to him, and he listened. When there was a specially tasty bone or juicy tidbit, she gave it to him in person. She had always loved him. Now he accepted that love, returned it. As I say, she became his woman.

Remembering Mike, we had wondered if Suzy had filled a need in Pat for a dog companion. Perhaps he had that need, and perhaps he had finally transferred that feeling, whatever it was, to us. Both of us. It had taken a long time, but there it was now, complete.

With that security, if I may reach over into a dubious area of psychology in discussing him, Pat resumed some of his earlier ways. I couldn't spend all my days roaming the mountain with him, even though I might have wished to, and when I was at my own work Pat often went on his own excursions. Not up on the mountain, but up and down the valley. He was the canine patriarch of the valley now. Poochy, old and ailing and finally helpless and miserable, had been mercifully put away. Teddy was long gone. Suzy was gone. Charley, like Albert, had a new pup. But Charley's pup as well as Albert's would have to live here a long time yet to own the valley, if they ever would own it.

Pat made his tours of his own domain. He went up to visit Charley, now and then, and to greet Elitha if she appeared. He never stayed, Charley said; just came and passed the time of day and told the pup that he still had a lot to learn. He went down to visit Albert and Ruth now and then, and to bristle in distant but sufficient recognition of Cubby's declaration of local sovereignty. But again, he never stayed more than a few minutes. He went on down the valley. Sometimes, on my way to the village, I saw him two miles from home, trotting along the roadside with that blandly proprietary air, making no show of either friendship or hostility to wayside dogs whom he must have known from previous years. He would hear my car, turn and look, wag his tail at me in recognition but totally without any interest in a ride, wait till I had passed, then continue on his way.

The snows came in late December. They came with some depth, enough to make my promised trip far up the mountain to look for snowshoe rabbits too arduous for either Pat or me. We prowled the pastures and the lower woodland from time to time, he investigating the state of the cottontail population, I watching for the tracks of the red fox that had been barking the moonlit hillside all fall. One day I found where the fox had walked one of the rails of the railroad track for nearly half a mile. There were his prints in the three inches of fresh snow on the rail, showing how he had fallen off three times but had persisted and finally had kept his balance several hundred yards without a slip. Pat couldn't understand why I was so interested in those tracks or that evidence of fox bravado, or whatever it was. He came and sniffed the tracks and as much as said, "I know that old bush-tail. He's been around several years." And he wandered off, looking for another rabbit.

The snow stayed on the ground. More snow came. The cold deepened. We both stayed indoors, and I wondered if Pat's blood might have begun to thin out. I thought he might wish to stay indoors at night, here in the warm house. But no, he still preferred his own bed, fresh air and all. Even with the wind roaring a gale and the snow coming down in eider blankets, he said that he wanted to be taken out to his own house. And was taken. And when I waded, knee-deep, to open his door in the morning, he came lunging out to wallow in the drifts like a porpoise in the sea, and to roll and slither and leap to his feet and bark his greeting to a new day. Pat still liked winter and snow.

But winters pass. March came, and then April, and the redbirds were whistling and the ducks were on the river and the robins stalked the pastures and the redwings *ka-reed* in all the boglands. Pat prowled the pastures for early woodchucks, and we planted peas, and all three of us got muddy to the knees.

May, and the violets were in bloom, the columbines in bud, the house wrens were building half a dozen nests at a time and singing as though theirs were the total responsibility for this world's song.

The boat was in the water. The vegetable garden was planted and the first crop of weeds hoed out. The flower beds were not yet the tangle of perennials and quack grass and dubious volunteer seedlings that makes me feel guilty if I take an hour off. And the worms were teeming in the lower end of the garden.

We went fishing. Pat went along.

Barbara caught a fifteen-inch brownie up by the island. I couldn't buy so much as a nibble. Pat was so exuberant he swam the river three times. Then I found a school of big, hungry perch and began to haul in the fish, and now Barbara couldn't even get a nibble, But she sat and jeered at me because I hadn't caught a trout. It was a wonderful afternoon to be alive and on the river.

Pat swam the river a fourth time and I said, "What does he think he is? A muskrat?" Then he waded along the shallows near the shore, frightening green frogs and nesting ducks and getting muddy as a catfish. "I can see right now," Barbara said, "that he'll have to be scrubbed before he can come in the house. That black mud is like tar, and we've just washed the rugs!" I said, "I'll take the rugs up. No house," I said, "especially a house in the country, should have rugs on the floor in the spring. Next thing, you'll make me take off my shoes before I come in." And she said, "Good idea."

It was an afternoon for laughter.

We fished, and we sensed, and we laughed with spring on the river, and we caught more fish than we needed. Then we started for home. Barbara insisted that I must weigh her brownie before I cleaned it. I promised. We stopped at a bank blue with wild forget-me-nots and I edged the boat in and I picked a bouquet, since they are Barbara's favorite flower. Except for violets, and apple blossoms, and columbines, and baby dahlias, and anemones and most of the others. That day, at least, they were her favorites.

We eased on down to the dock. I secured the boat, helped Barbara onto the float. And she said, "Where's Pat?" I hadn't thought of Pat. I said, "He'll be along. He's still frightening frogs, probably." And I took the string of fish to the old fish-sink beside the garage and began cleaning them.

I was almost through cleaning fish when I heard Pat howl. It was a pain howl. Then there was silence. I waited and listened. I heard him again. He was barking now, and howling too. The "Where are you Boss" barking. Somewhere up the river.

I hurried toward the house. Barbara had come out on the porch. "Isn't that Pat?" she asked. "Yes," I said. "I'm going up and see what's wrong." She urged, "Hurry!"

I loped down to the float, pulled the cover back just enough to get in, cast off, jerked the starter rope and gunned the motor. I went roaring upstream, shouting as I went. Pat heard me and answered, his yelps peremptory now.

It was early dusk. Half a dozen black ducks took fright and beat the water to a froth as they winged away, up the river. Somewhere back in the woods a wood thrush was calling in that lovely, peaceful contralto, and beyond him were two mourning doves calling. A strangely peaceful evening. A lovely evening.

I shouted again, and Pat answered, just ahead, on the far side of the river. I put the boat over, rounded a big clump of alder brush, and there he was, lying on a grassy bank. I called and he whined, and he got to his feet, then lay down again. His right forefoot was caught in something. I slid the boat inshore, grabbed the painter in one hand and jumped out. Into black mud that sucked at my feet, oozed up around my calves. I waded up the bank onto the grass. And found Pat caught in a muskrat trap. Some fool trapping muskrats there the previous fall had failed to take up that trap when he ended the season. It lay there, set and chained to a deep-driven peg on the bank, all winter. And Pat, sloshing in the shallows, had stepped into it.

I knelt, saw that it had him by two toes, and thanked heaven that it wasn't a mink trap or a fox trap, but a relatively light muskrat trap. I tromped on its spring and released him. Then I jerked up the peg and flung peg, chain and trap far out into the deep water, damning all trappers.

Pat whined his gratitude and licked his paw. I examined it as best I could in the dim light. No bones seemed to be broken. He got to his feet and scrambled back up the bank on three legs. I ordered him back, and he came, and I took him in my arms and put him in the boat. I got in, and we came home, I muddy as a ditch swamper, Pat looking like something hauled out of a flooded coal mine.

Barbara was waiting on the porch. "Is he all right?" she called as we came up the walk, Pat still on three legs.

"Got his toes pinched in a muskrat trap!" I said.

"Is he *hurt*?"

"I don't know!"

She held the door wide. We trailed in, still dripping. Pat plopped down and I crouched beside him and went over the injured foot. Pat watched me with a sheepish look. The foot was bruised and there was an ooze of blood around one nail, but there were no broken bones, not even an open cut. At last I stood up and said, "No damage. He'll be all right in a few days."

Barbara had watched, tense. Now she exclaimed, "Thank goodness! I had visions of another dash to the vet, or even worse." Then she looked at me, she looked at Pat, and she looked at the rug. "Get out of here!" she said. "Both of you! Go give him a bath, and take one yourself!" Then she laughed. "My nice clean rug. Well, thank goodness it *is* washable."

Pat limped around for a week. But the limp didn't check his riverbank prowls when we went fishing, though I noticed that he was wary of the shallows and hadn't much interest in frogs. And it didn't much impede his woodchuck forays. But the woodchuck battles were less frequent now. Pat had cleaned out most of the chucks in the pastures. Now and then he went up onto the lower mountainside and I heard his battle cry and he came home with a trophy to ripen in the sun. But the only woodchuck in sight of the house, the only one we saw at all regularly at least, was old Gramp up there at the Resting Rock.

I still wonder if Gramp and Pat hadn't reached some sort of arrangement. They were both patriarchs, after all. If there wasn't a deal between them, they had reached a state of mutual skill that resulted in a draw. Whatever their status, Pat spent hours stalking Gramp and Gramp spent hours taunting Pat, and Gramp always reached his rock-bound den a jump ahead of Pat.

Spring flowered into summer and Pat gave up on Gramp, except for an occasional afternoon challenge. He moved his operations up the road, to the Trestle Lot, brought home four chucks from up there and seemed to have cleaned out that field too. I thought he would take a little time off after that and just enjoy life's June leisure. But not Pat.

We were eating lunch one late June day, all the windows open, when I heard the woodchuck battle cry in the distance. Or something that sounded like it. I glanced at Barbara and she nodded and smiled. I thought that in another hour or so he would be at home, napping on the front steps, and I would go out and find his trophy in the driveway by the garage. We went on eating.

But that distant battle cry continued. It increased in urgency. Finally I went out on the front porch and listened. It sounded across the river and upstream. I shouted, "Pat! Get him, Pat! Go in and get him!"

The echo died away, and Pat yelped louder than ever. He had heard me. He was calling, "Hey, Boss! Come help!"

I came back in and took down the .22 rifle. Barbara asked where I was going and I told her what I had heard. "Maybe he's got a bobcat," she suggested. "Maybe he's treed one."

"Could be," I said. "I'm going up there and see."

There isn't a good landing place for the boat over there, so I walked up the road to the railroad track and crossed the river on the trestle, shouting to Pat from time to time. He kept yelping back that he had something cornered. I cut down through the tangle of undergrowth to a patch of scrubby pines, and there was Pat, yelping at something he had treed. I worked in closer, and there was a whopping big woodchuck fifteen feet up a pine tree. The limbs grew close together and the chuck had gone up, apparently, as it might have climbed a ladder. It was hunched in a crotch, glaring and snapping its jaws. I shot it and it came down in a heap and Pat made sure it was dead. I praised him properly and ordered him back to the trestle with me. He went, reluctantly. But at the trestle he balked. Walk that thing? Never! He stood there watching while I made my way across, and then he went down to the river, waded in and swam over to join me. We came home.

That afternoon we went fishing. Pat seemed more than usually eager to go along, and he swam the river at the first chance. He prowled in the brush, out of sight, most of the time we fished. Finally we drifted back down toward the dock, to come in.

We had just passed the trestle when I saw Pat come down to the water's edge with a woodchuck in his mouth. A whopper of a chuck, bigger, I thought, than the one he had treed and I had shot for him. It was so big he half dragged it. I said, "So, he's got another one. Found virgin territory over there, apparently."

We watched as he came down the river, looked around, then made his way to the next opening in the brush. There he took a firmer grip on the big chuck, dragged it into the water till it was water-borne. Barbara exclaimed, "He isn't going to try to swim the river with that thing!"

"I guess he is," I said, and I started the motor, just in case he needed help.

But he needed no help from me. He knew what he was doing. He swam confidently, but slowly, across the river, pushing that woodchuck ahead of him like a tug pushing a barge. He chose his landing, waded ashore, laid down his cargo and caught his breath. Then he picked it up again and half carried, half dragged it up the bank and across the road into the upper pasture.

We came on down, docked, and carried our gear up from the boat. I was fileting the fish when Pat appeared, strutting. His nose was brown with dirt, and his forepaws were muddied. There was no doubt what he had done. He had taken his big chuck into the pasture, chosen a bare spot somewhere, dug a hole, and buried it to ripen.

I write a column once a week for the daily newspaper in Pittsfield, Massachusetts, a column mostly about country matters. For the next week I wrote a column about Pat, telling a little of his history and his achievements and concluding with the story of his treed woodchuck and his swim with that big one in his mouth. Pat had appeared in the column before, so he was known to the readers by name at least. But this time the editor wanted to use a picture of him with the column. The picture was provided and the column appeared, picture and all.

The day after the column was in print I had a telephone call from Great Barrington. A woman's voice. "You have our dog!" she exclaimed. "I know, from the picture, and he sounds just like our dog."

I was astonished. I asked when they lost their dog. The date she gave me didn't tally, by several months, with Pat's arrival here. I asked a few other questions, but my caller said, "It doesn't matter. Really it doesn't. My husband doesn't know I called, and he would be mad if he knew about it, but I just had to call and know he's all right!"

"Of course he's all right," I said. "And if he's your dog, come on down and—well, we'll do something about it. Give me your name, and I'll—"

But she had hung up.

I told Barbara. She said, "I don't believe it! We advertised him, and— When did she say they lost him?"

I told her.

"April! Why, he came here on Christmas night!"

"O.K.," I said. "So she's mistaken. They lost a black and white dog. Years ago. Now she sees a picture of a black and white dog, and—"

I remembered the time we sent Pat away, over to New York State, and he came back here. I remembered all the other times he could have gone back to an earlier home, and didn't. It all seemed too circumstantial.

"Forget it," I said. "She said it didn't matter. And she didn't give me her name."

"If it does matter, she'll call again."

"Yes."

"And we'll have to ask her down."

"Yes."

"And then she'll know she's mistaken."

"Then she'll know," I said.

CHAPTER 16

T HE WOMAN didn't call again. I decided it was one of those instances where someone loses a dog and later sees a picture of a dog the same color and is sure it must be the one she lost. Memory is fallible and can be shaped to hope's convenience. The fact that Pat was a homeless dog when he came to us made this woman's hope not only plausible but inevitably true, to her. But, charitable as I might be, I couldn't get around the fact that Pat was not a woman's dog and, as far as I could see, never had been.

So the woman must be mistaken. I wished there was something I could do about it. I thought of putting a note in my column asking her to send me her name so that I could go and see her, perhaps take Pat along so she could see him and know she was mistaken. But that seemed cruel. If, as seemed inevitable, he wasn't the dog she had lost the old wound would be reopened, the hurt and the remembering. She had said it didn't matter now. Perhaps it was better to let the situation lie. If it did matter to her, she would call again.

Barbara and I discussed it and I decided to wait.

Ten days later we were eating supper and Pat was lying in the living room when I heard a car come down the road and pull into our driveway. Pat growled and began to bark, his "Strangers are here" bark. I told Pat to quiet down and went to the front door. Pat came and stood bristling beside me.

A man got out of the car and came up the walk, a big, pleasant-faced man in work clothes. He came onto the porch and stopped and stared at Pat, inside the screen door with me, and he smiled. He said, "Hello," and he told me his name. I didn't recognize it. He said, "My wife phoned you last week. I had to come to see the dog." He looked at Pat again, and he said, "That's him." He drew a sigh, as though a long wait had ended.

I invited him in. Pat sniffed at him, still bristling, and the man said, "Hello, Skippy." Pat made no response and I told him to go lie down. He went, reluctantly, and lay down on his rug in the living room, watching the man suspiciously.

Barbara came and I introduced them, and she asked the man to have supper with us. No, he said, he had eaten. But he would have a cup of coffee while we finished eating. So we went out to the dining porch and sat down.

Barbara got coffee for him and I said, "Tell me about your dog."

"Well," he said, and he hesitated. "It's quite a while back," he finally went on. "But when that picture was in the paper, and what you wrote about him, my wife saw it and she was sure it was Skippy. So she called you, and then she thought she shouldn't have called, and she didn't want to make any trouble, so she hung up on you. And the next day she told me and showed me the picture. And—well, I just had to come and see for myself." He smiled. "She doesn't know I'm here. I don't want her to know. Not now, anyway."

He sipped his coffee and he looked at his hands, the strong hands of a workman. He thought for several minutes, then said, "We were hunting rabbits, a friend and I, over in Monterey. Skippy was the best rabbit dog I ever had, one of the best I ever saw. It was a mean day, raw and cold and spitting snow."

"When was this?" I asked.

"Let's see. Seven years ago. Seven years last winter."

"What month?"

"Gosh, it's hard to say. February, I think. Could have been earlier than that, though. Maybe December, but it seems like it was February."

I nodded. "Go on."

"Well, we hunted all afternoon. It was a Saturday. He put up plenty of rabbits, and they really ran. It was getting late and I said we'd get just one more, then go home before the roads got too bad. And Skip put one up and went up the mountain, up into one of those birch hollows. And he didn't come back. We waited around there for an hour, hollering and calling, and finally I went up the hollow and my friend stayed on the stand. And not a sign of old Skipper. Not a yelp. Then it began to get dark and we had to go home."

He drew a long sigh and waited and drank another gulp of coffee. "I went back there the next day," he said. "Spent all afternoon on that mountain, looking for him. And there wasn't a sign, not a trace of him."

He paused again, and looked at me, then looked away. "I went over there every weekend, looking. For months, every time I was over that way I looked, hoping I wouldn't find a pile of bones and a patch of black and white hair. Hoping, to tell the truth, that somebody else had found him and given him a good home. You hate to think a dog got caught in a trap, maybe, or in the rocks somewhere and just—well, just died. You like to know, one way or another. That's why I had to come down here tonight."

We had finished eating. We all went into the living room. Pat glanced up, then lay back and napped again. The man stared at him and slowly shook his head. "I still can't believe it. It's like seeing a ghost. But every mark's right. I've got snapshots at home I could show you."

Barbara said, "When your wife called, she talked as though it was her dog that was lost."

He smiled. "You know how it is. She raised him. I got him as a puppy and she raised him, housebroke him, taught him his manners."

"With a broom?" Barbara asked.

"No! With a rolled-up newspaper. She loved him, darn near made a house dog out of him. And he thought the world of her. But he had beagle blood in him, a nose. I made a rabbit dog out of him."

"You say he had beagle blood?" I asked.

"Beagle and foxhound. His mother was a blooded beagle and his father was a black and white hound. He took after his father." He looked at Pat. "He's got a white spot about the size of a half a dollar on his right hip, right? That hip's all black except that one little white spot."

Pat was lying on his right side. I spoke to him, ordered him to get up. He got to his feet, came to me. I knew the spot was there.

"There!" the man exclaimed. "There it is!"

I told Pat to lie down again.

Pat lay down facing the man. He said, "He's getting old. Grizzled around the muzzle. His brows used to be coal black. Frosty-looking now." He shook his head. "When he was just a pup the kids played with him all the time. Threw a ball for him to chase, that kind of thing. And he followed them all over town on their bikes."

"Your kids had bicycles?" I asked.

"Sure. What kid hasn't?"

"Pat hates bicycles."

"What?"

"He hates bicycles. He doesn't chase cars, but he hates bicycles."

"That's funny. I wonder what happened to change him that way." Then he said, "But just let me show him a gun and he forgot the kids, and the balls and everything else. He loved to go hunting. If I didn't take him out, he went on his own, after woodchucks, just like you wrote. We've got a place something like yours, situated like yours, a mountain in back. He ran that mountainside and cleaned out the woodchucks. Lord knows how many he killed." Then he laughed. "And cats! You don't have cats, do you? Not with him around!"

"No," I said, "we haven't any cats. Never did have. Now and then a big tom from up the road comes down and spends a week or so in the big barn, cleaning out the rats and a few of the squirrels."

"And I'll bet Skip—the dog—makes it hot for him."

"This is a pretty wise old tom, and fast on his feet. They seem to get along as long as the cat doesn't come into the dooryard."

"He's changed, then. The cats I buried! I had a private graveyard for cats that he killed. It got so that I hated to face the neighbors when I came home at night. Every time someone got a new cat, he put it out of business. There was one big old tom down the street that held out quite a while. Skipper put him up a tree pretty near every day, though, and he finally got him. That was one thing I never could break him of, killing cats."

"Did you ever try to run coons with him?"

"Coons? No. He never seemed interested, and I didn't push him. I never knew a good rabbit dog that would run coons. Not unless he'd run everything that came along."

"I've heard that cat-killers make good coon dogs."

"I don't know. All I know is that he never ran coons. Does he now?"

"No . . . How long did you have Skippy? How old was he when you lost him, over there in Monterey?"

"How old? Oh, let's see. A little over six years old."

"And when was it you lost him?"

"Seven years ago. Seven years last winter." He looked at Pat, then turned to me. "That would make him thirteen! Thirteen years old!" There was awe in his voice. "No wonder he's getting grizzled. That's getting old, for a dog."

"Tell me," I said, "did he like to swim?"

"Swim? Sure. He swam when he had to, and he didn't seem to

184

mind it. Pretty good swimmer. Not like a Chesapeake or a spaniel, but— I never tried to get him to retrieve. Have you?"

"No. I don't hunt ducks."

"I thought there were ducks on the river, down this way."

"There are, a few. But I don't hunt them. We fish the river."

"Pretty dirty, isn't it? Not many fish."

"It's not very bad down here," I said. "From Barrington up it's filthy, I know, but it's reasonably clean by the time it gets down here. If you fellows up in Massachusetts would do something about it, you could have a decent river up there too, instead of an open sewer. But nobody seems to care. . . . You said you had kids. And they were fond of the dog."

"They're grown up, now. Anyway, he was my dog, not theirs. Mine, and the wife's. She raised him, and I trained him." He looked at me, and he said, "I didn't come down to get him. I just had to come see. You know how it is. And to see if he had a good home, and—" He hesitated, and I saw the fight going on in him. You have a dog, and you lose him, and you keep wondering. Then you see a dog that you're sure is the dog you lost. You think maybe it could be the same as it used to be, you and your dog, and you know it can't. The years come between you. But there's the tug at your memory, and your heart, the wish to recover that man-dog relationship again.

It was all there in his face. I'd have been the same way, and I knew it. I'd have said the same thing. "I didn't come down to get him." And yet I would wish I could have him again, have the dog I used to have, and make the years drop away.

It's a hard decision, hard all around.

And I knew, too, that I didn't want to wreck it all for him. He was sure he had found his lost Skippy, the dog he didn't want to die alone, trapped out in the hills somewhere. He had pestered himself for weeks, months, maybe still did, with the thought that if he'd stayed just another half hour, that raw, sleety winter evening, his dog might have come back. And now he had found an answer that he could accept and make an end to his pestering. He could live with that answer and be content, just to know in his own heart that Pat was the lost Skippy.

I couldn't wreck that.

But the questions kept pestering. At me.

The wife who raised and housebroke that dog and taught him manners; if she didn't use a broom on him, who did? And if he loved that woman, why was he so wary of women, all women, when he came here? Why did it take him so long to accept Barbara and show deep affection for her? And if he grew up with kids who rode bicycles, why did he hate bicycles now?

If he was lost in the Monterey area, why did he come all the way down here instead of going back to Great Barrington? Barrington was closer than Weatogue Valley, miles closer. And when we sent him away, over to that York State farm, why did he come back here instead of to Barrington, which again was closer?

If he was a cat-killer, why had he made a kind of truce with that big old tom out in the big barn, instead of killing him? Why was he content to run that cat up an apple tree now and then and warn him to stay out of the dooryard? On the other hand, did he have that battle with the bobcat up on the mountain when he first came here because he hated cats? And did that fight cure him of the old cat-killing urge?

The questions, the nagging questions. And no real answers.

The man's evidence was mixed. Some of his details were persuasive, and some just didn't add up. Then I thought of myself sitting there, say seven years hence, trying to remember Pat the way he is at this moment. There would be gaps in my memory, lapses and contradictions. I tried to remember whether Mike had three white paws, or four, and for the life of me I couldn't decide.

I asked the man, "You only had the one dog?"

"That's right. Just Skipper."

"Was there another dog along that day you lost him on the mountain?"

"No. When we took Skip out for rabbits we never needed another dog. Why?"

"Well," I persisted, "was there a little black dog in your neighborhood, a pup that might have had setter blood?"

He shook his head, baffled. "No."

"Pat wasn't traveling alone when he came here," I said. "This other dog was with him. Pat seemed to be looking after him. They came together, the same night, and we took them both in. We had to get rid of the black one. Gave him away."

The man shook his head again. "I can't figure that one. Skip didn't run with any other dog, and there wasn't any dog like that anywhere around." He stared at Pat, and he said, "I see he's got a slit ear. Was it that way when he came here?"

"No. He tangled with a bobcat, up on the mountain."

"Kill him?"

"I think so. I wasn't there. He got pretty well clawed up."

The man smiled. "I told you he was a cat-killer." Then he sighed. "Well, I'd better be getting along. The wife'll wonder where I am. Sorry to have bothered you this way, and I certainly don't want to make any trouble. But I had to come and see for myself. You understand?"

"I understand. I'd do the same thing. I'm glad you came. You know," I said, "it always seemed to me that there are two kinds of dogs. There are dogs that a man owns, and there are dogs that own a man. I think he's that kind of dog."

He looked at me, surprised. He thought for a second and said, "I guess you're right, at that. Some dogs you never do own, do you? They own you. I guess they pick you out, or something. Skip was that kind."

There was a moment's silence. Then Barbara said, "Why don't we let Pat pick now?"

The man looked at her, frowning.

"Go ahead," she urged. "Call him to you. Let's just see."

He drew a deep breath and looked at Pat, and he said, "Skipper. Skip! Come here, Skip." It was a quiet order, the way a man speaks to a dog he has known a long time and still cherishes.

I held my breath, watching, waiting.

Pat didn't move, didn't open an eye. I heard Barbara let out a held breath.

The man glanced at me and slowly shook his head.

Barbara turned to me. "You call him."

I said, "Pat," and he opened an eye, lifted his head. I said, "Come here, Pat," and held out my hand.

Slowly, stiffly, Pat got to his feet. He came over and nosed my hand. He looked up at me, questioning, and slowly wagged his tail.

The man sighed and got to his feet.

I went with him to the door. Pat followed us. The man remembered and turned to Barbara and said, "Thanks for the coffee, ma'am," and he shook hands with me. He looked down at Pat, but he didn't even put a hand on him.

We went out onto the porch and he went down the steps. At the bottom he said, "Take good care of him," and he crossed the grass to his car and got in and drove back the way he had come.

Pat went out and looked around, smelled where the car had been, and I came back inside.

Barbara said, "You don't think Pat *is* his dog, do you?"

"I don't know. Maybe he was, once."

"He couldn't be! Didn't you see all the contradictions in what he said? He didn't even lose his dog till after Pat came here!"

"I don't know," I said again. "It was seven years ago. A man forgets."

Pat was at the door, asking to be let in. I opened the door for him. "Well, Skipper?" I said.

He looked up at me and wagged his tail. I glanced at Barbara. She said, "Well, Stinky?"

He looked at her and wagged his tail. She laughed.

I said, "Pat, go lie down on your rug." He went.

We went into the kitchen and began clearing away from supper. As she scraped the scraps into Pat's food bowl for tomorrow Barbara said, "Do you know what really made him decide the way he did?"

"Who?"

"Pat."

"What?"

"I don't use a broom on him!"

"So now *you* think he is Skipper?"

"Well, if he was Skipper, and if he did remember—" She broke off. "It isn't funny, is it? Did you see the look on that poor man's face when he called Pat and he didn't make a move? And then he went right to you."

"I saw it."

"I almost wanted to cry." Then she said, "You're right. People don't own dogs. Not dogs like Pat. Pat owns us. He picked us, and now he owns us."

We finished cleaning up, and it was nine o'clock. I went into the living room and said, "How about it, Pat? Bedtime."

He got to his feet, stretched and went ahead of me to the door.

We went outside and he sniffed the cool night air flowing gently down off the mountain. He stood there sniffing it and a whippoorwill called from the far edge of the pasture. Pat started toward the mountain, lured by some enticing scent. I called to him, sharply. "Come back here! None of that nonsense. Off to bed with you, you grizzled old reprobate."

He came, reluctantly, and he trotted ahead of me to his house, tail high, nose alert. He paused at the doorway and looked at the mountain again and sniffed the darkness. Then he went inside and I closed and latched the door.

I turned back toward the house, where Barbara was putting out the downstairs lights. I stopped under the big apple tree and the night air stirred the leaves to a rustling whisper. I looked up the mountain and smelled the night, almost as Pat had done. And I thought of that man, driving home alone with his memories. But with peace in his heart, at last, about the dog he called Skipper. The dog that he was now sure didn't die, trapped and alone, on that mountainside up in Monterey. A man has to know.

Then I came inside.

POSTSCRIPT

I T IS MARCH as I write this, early March, and we have just had the deepest snowfall of the winter, as often happens here in these old hills. Last week it was like spring, the brooks laughing and chattering, bank-full, and the river flowing free and dark. The first flock of black ducks had returned to the river, and I was watching for the migrant robins which come and stalk the pasture in flocks of a hundred or more. Pat was out, sniffing at all the old dens to see if any woodchucks were out looking for mates after their long sleep. He didn't find any. The woodchucks know what time it is, just as the robins do. And as I should have known.

It began to snow before daylight yesterday. It snowed all day, and if the temperature had been twenty degrees lower it would have been a blizzard. As it was, the drifts piled up, four and five feet deep. When I put Pat to bed last night I had to wade through snow up to my knees, and he had to follow in my tracks. The storm continued well into the night. But when I got up this morning the sky was clear, the stars brilliant, the wind dying. And the temperature was down close to zero.

I avoided the deep drifts when I went to let Pat out, but I still waded through drifts over my knees. And when I looked at the river it was only a winding white highway, iced over again and covered with snow, the third freeze-up and the one that is supposed to close the book on winter for another year. When this ice goes out, tradition says, spring will come.

Pat heard me coming and barked his impatience. When I opened the door he came out with a rush—and buried himself to his ears in that first lunge. He shook his head and barked in delight, and he dived headfirst into an even deeper drift and began to roll, ecstatic. He rolled and snorted and rolled again, and he jumped to his feet and sneezed the snow from his nose and blinked it from his eyelashes and stood there in the rising sun, shimmering from nose to tail. Then he dolphined his way across the yard in great lunges to the road, where the snowplow had already carved a shallow canyon. He sniffed here and there, nosed the tair, and trotted down the road in the dazzling crispness of a new day to investigate the state of his world. He was gone almost an hour before he barked at the door and came in and demanded his breakfast.

I shoveled out the walks and opened the way to the garage, and Pat lay in the sun on the front porch steps watching me. When I had finished he came indoors and up to my study with me. We have been here two hours, he napping and dreaming and twitching his paws and uttering little muffled yelps of excitement.

In a few more weeks I shall go down to the town clerk's office and renew his license and get a new brass tag for his collar. The clerk will flip open her record book and say, "Pat? Still the same dog?"

I will say yes, still Pat.

She will find the page and start filling in the blank, reading as she writes. "Pat . . . Black and white foxhound . . . Age?" She will hesitate. She always does. She will leaf back. "Let's see. He was four years old the first time you registered him. That was eight years ago. I guess that makes him twelve now, doesn't it?"

"Better keep the record consistent," I will say.

She will write it down that way, "Age, 12." And we will have our joke, the same joke we have had for the past three years.

"You want to apply for Social Security for him? He's old enough."

"Pat never did a day's work in his life. He'll have to wait till I apply for mine."

We will laugh and I will pay the fee and take the new brass tag and bring it home and fasten it on Pat's collar. He will scratch his neck to hear it jingle. Then he will go to the door and ask to be let out. It will be April. Woodchucks will be out, maybe old Gramp sunning himself on the Resting Rock. Pat will have to go and see. After all, this is his valley, his mountainside, his world. . . .

He is dreaming again, twitching and uttering those excited, muffled yelps. He has wakened himself. He looks at me, puzzled for an instant as though not sure where he is, then looks abashed and turns away. I wonder if he was dreaming about last spring, or last fall, or of the spring and fall ahead. Or if it was a dream about a sleety winter day on a mountainside up in Monterey.

I don't know. I still don't know.

And does it matter? Must life be all of a piece? I doubt it. Mine hasn't been. I, too, made my choices.